W9-ANI-739

ALSO BY ERIC G. WILSON

Everyone Loves a Good Train Wreck:
Why We Can't Look Away

Against Happiness: In Praise of Melancholy

KEEP IT FAKE

KEEP IT FAKE

Inventing

an Authentic

Life

ERIC G. WILSON

SARAH CRICHTON BOOKS
Farrar, Straus and Giroux | *New York*

Sarah Crichton Books
Farrar, Straus and Giroux
18 West 18th Street, New York 10011

Library of Congress Cataloging-in-Publication Data
Wilson, Eric, 1967–
    Keep it fake : inventing an authentic life / Eric G. Wilson. —
First edition.
        pages   cm
    Includes bibliographical references and index.
    ISBN 978-0-374-18102-4 (cloth : alk. paper) —
    ISBN 978-0-374-70947-1 (e-book : alk. paper)
    1. Sincerity.   2. Reality in literature.   3. Truthfulness and
falsehood.   4. Wilson, Eric, 1967– —Philosophy.   5. Authors,
American—Biography.   I. Title.

BJ1533.S55W55 2015
177'.3—dc23

                                                    2014029305

Designed by Abby Kagan

Farrar, Straus and Giroux books may be purchased for educational,
business, or promotional use. For information on bulk purchases, please
contact the Macmillan Corporate and Premium Sales Department at
1-800-221-7945, extension 5442, or write to specialmarkets@macmillan.com.

www.fsgbooks.com
www.twitter.com/fsgbooks • www.facebook.com/fsgbooks

1   3   5   7   9   10   8   6   4   2

For Phil Arnold, a sleight-of-hand man

The crude commercialism of America, its materialising spirit, its indifference to the poetical side of things, and its lack of imagination and of high unattainable ideals, are entirely due to that country having adopted for its national hero a man who, according to his own confession, was incapable of telling a lie, and it is not too much to say that the story of George Washington and the cherry-tree has done more harm, and in a shorter space of time, than any other moral tale in the whole of literature.

—OSCAR WILDE

Everyone wants to be Cary Grant—even I want to be Cary Grant.

—CARY GRANT

It was hilarious, regardless of reality.

—ANONYMOUS INTERVIEWEE ON *ENTERTAINMENT TONIGHT*

KEEP IT FAKE

1.

I am the boy whose first word was "ball." I am six and sitting at dinner with my parents and two-year-old brother. We are eating chicken-and-cream-of-mushroom casserole, Del Monte green beans, and Brown 'n Serve dinner rolls. On the Zenith in the other room, Cronkite drones, "And that's the way it was." The overhead bulbs glare on the pine-green plates and the charred candlewicks we light only on steak nights. Earlier that day, my best friend, John, had said that his first word was "bubba." We found this funny, since the only man we knew by this name was a limping three-hundred-pounder who stank and cackled while draining thirty-footers during the half-times of junior high basketball games. I didn't know my first word. So I asked that night. My mom was pouring iced tea, and Dad was reaching for the butter, and they said, in unison, "ball." This was the best response ever.

Dad, still wearing his whistle at the table, was the head football coach at the local high school. The game consumed him, and he passed the obsession to me. In my childhood photographs, I'm wearing football jerseys in all colors; the number always falls between five and fifteen, a quarterback-favoring range. I'm also hugging NFL-size footballs. By the age of five, I'm already collecting Topps trading cards of pro players, though I don't yet possess a picture of my favorite, Fran Tarkenton, the quarterback of the Minnesota Vikings. The coach makes up for this by giving me a Tarkenton jersey for Christmas, purple polyester, white number ten, gold and white stripes on the sleeves, and, best of all, printed on the back, spanning my shoulder blades, "Wilson." This begins a holiday tradition, lasting until the eighth grade: a new jersey of a new favorite QB. Joe Namath one year, Terry Bradshaw another, Ken Stabler, Dan Pastorini, Steve Bartkowski, Jim Zorn, and Tommy Kramer (Tarkenton's replacement) on yet others. And always along with the jersey comes a fresh football. I can wear out a pigskin in a year, easy. If I'm awake and not at school, I'm passing, kicking, punting. By the time I'm six, I lie in bed just before lights-out and throw the ball toward the ceiling over and over, each time imagining I am Fran, and each toss and catch, a touchdown.

"Ball" proved prophetic: I spent my early childhood training to be a quarterback, played the position well on my middle school's team, played it better in high school—leading the '83 team to the school's only undefeated regular season—and ended up being recruited by West Point to play for Army.

Only when I hit the U.S. Military Academy on July 1, 1985, and questioned quarterbacking and everything else, did I doubt my parents' honesty. There was no way I really blurted that word. Surely the coach *wanted* so much for my first word to be "ball" that he translated my blubbery random *b*'s and *l*'s into his favorite sound. Doing so, with my agreeable mom cheering on, he thrust me into a narrative, with a beginning, middle, and end satisfying to his soul: "My boy was born to the gridiron."

What if he had converted my babble into "ma-ma" or "da-da" or "dog" or "duck" or "car"? Would I be crashing in derbies or blasting mallards or suffering serious Freud lashings? (Which I actually am.) What if I'd said poor John's first word and found myself shuffling around gyms fat, lonely, and mocked? John escaped this destiny, became fast, lean, and popular and cool and got all the girls my neurotic self (is "Hamlet" ever a first word?) never could. His parents didn't make a big deal, I guess, over "bubba." They eased him into other plots, loose and casual, and so his narrative was open-ended, more *Tristram Shandy* than my *Great Expectations*.

Regardless of form, digressive or linear, by the time we become aware of ourselves we are already trapped in fictions not of our making, and our only hope of escaping the text is to write our way into stories of our own. Our self-fashioned narrative, however, no matter how original, has already been determined by the tale we inherited: we can only define ourselves somewhere on a spectrum running from "fuck you, old man" to "I'm a chip off the old block." Whether I become a footballer, a poet, a doper, or live fast and leave a fine corpse, I am always the boy who first said "ball."

More goes into a self than grammar, syntax, semantics, plot: atoms violently birthed in the Big Bang, the make of our species, millennia of history and culture, DNA. Each of us is a braid whose strands range from the oldest hemp to most recent nylon. But only one line elevates us from mere being to abundant meaning, from bare existence that is what it is, nothing more, to purpose, yearning, failure, love, writing books, and comparing cell phones. That line is language.

At the dinner table that night in '73, encased in our rancher in tiny Taylorsville, North Carolina, my dad, my mom, my brother, and I: we were all informed by stories ancient and near: the biblical myths, the parables of American Christianity, dreams of the Democratic Party, Southern gothic lore, small-town tales, the fantasy scripts of parents, our own earliest gurgles and coos. We were (and are) each a node in a vast textual network, crisscrossed by thousands of narratives, out of which we in our own way were (are) trying, fated and desperate, to weave a cogent "I."

How many moments have you lived so far? Ten years contain about five million, so do the calculations. (I'm somewhere between twenty and twenty-five million myself.) How many things have happened to you during those minutes, or have you made happen? Billions and billions. When you piece together an identity, a story of who you are, you choose only a fraction of these events as components of the narrative, a narrative already determined by millions of preexisting ones, and you emphasize some episodes over others and slant the tale to support your idea of self.

You find yourself a character of a great gloomy luminous novel composed for you for untold centuries, and you labor most of your days to seize the pen for yourself, form your own plot, grow into your heart's hero. The work is in progress: you revise earlier passages to conform to your current feelings. You do the same with the present moment, altering your self-definition in the "now" to correspond to memory's eruptions.

2.

The snuffed candle around which my family and I were huddled that night might as well have been a fire; our wood-paneled walls, cave rock; and our artifice-making, painted images flickering on those walls, alive. Tens of thousands of years ago, when the language among Homo sapiens sounded little different from an infant's grunting, men and women first discovered how representations of material existence—paintings, words, shadows—can shape physical experiences. This event marks a decisive move from animal to human, from rut and devour to brooding on the quick and the dead.

In *Cave of Forgotten Dreams*, his documentary on the Chauvet Cave in southern France, Werner Herzog considers the purpose of the thirty-thousand-year-old paintings on the cave's walls, the rhinos, hyenas, horses, panthers, cows, mammoths, lions, bears. The fires that burned near these creatures were not for cooking. They were for shadows. Standing between the flames and the wall, the cave folk could watch their own figures blend with the animal ones and imagine the beasts moving within the gestures of their human forms. For Herzog, this was Paleolithic cinema, and it reminded him of Fred Astaire in *Swing Time*, in which the dancer's shadows break loose and start their own tapping, which Fred in the flesh rushes to follow.

Shadows and stories alike seem to arise from substances, facts. But the image and the narrative in turn determine how stuff appears: how it signifies, what its value is. A fake rhino flickering orange and black in the cavern can be, as a symbol of human fear and desire, more real—more intense, more meaningful—than the one in the wild. And a single word, like a lodestone, might pull the scattered filings of a life into glimmering symmetries.

This idea restores balance in our scientific and materialist society, where one sees to believe. Belief, as well, dictates seeing. The mind may be a mirror, quietly reflecting the data, but it is also a lamp. It lightens or shades what it looks upon.

But what if this balance is a myth? What if there is *only* the lantern, only belief, if we never find but instead *create* the world, if Fred Astaire (né Frederic Austerlitz) knew in his shimmering film what is *truly* true: shadows are in charge?

Neuroscientists, psychologists, sociologists, philosophers, poets, novelists, and filmmakers have asserted the primacy of shades. There is no stable, accessible reality *out there* on which we can base objectively valid claims. Whether our left brains are shaping the raw data of our right into fabulous stories, or our unconscious assumptions about what should be true pervert facts into wish fulfillment, or we are so saturated in society's conventions that we're always acting out prefab scripts, or modern capitalism secretly (and perniciously) seduces us into turning ourselves into homogenized commodities, we can't help living in fiction.

3.

On the surface, this, if true, is apocalyptic. Forget our reality-obsessed clichés. *Keep it real. Shoot straight from the hip. Be all that you can be. Keep it on the level. It is what it is. Tell it like it is. Wherever you go, there you are. I feel you. Welcome to the real world. He's the real deal.* Forget, too, the cinema icons of laconic honesty: Gary Cooper or Frank Capra's James Stewart; Rhett Butler pulling back Scarlett's veils; Clint Eastwood slicing through the shit; Forrest Gump, who compensates for his dumbness with his inability to fib; those feisty women, too: Norma Rae, Erin Brockovich, Ridley Scott's Ripley. Put aside as well the sacred distinction between truth-telling leaders—Washington, who cannot lie, Honest Abe—and all those scoundrels, the Slick Willies, the Tricky Dicks.

This is all small stuff. The real crisis of reality's flight would be the loss of Being itself (who knows what is what if it's all made up?), Knowledge (fantasy vanquishes fact, and what's left but collective dream?), Morality (in reverie, how do you tell good from ill?), and Beauty (aren't one person's fabricated standards of pulchritude as valid as another's?). We all would be trapped in a chamber of infinite mirrors, some of our own sanding, others made by Lord knows whom, with no single image proving intrinsically superior to any other, and where *anything* goes, and everything *goes*: the love you thought was real, and the charm of your lovely daughter (name of Una), and the ecstasy upon witnessing the last scene of Woody Allen's (Allen Stewart Konigsberg's) *Manhattan*, the martini's chilled rush, E. M. Forster ("only connect"), D. H. Lawrence's "Bavarian Gentians," Etruscan roads near Orvieto, arugula, the weirdness of William Wordsworth, and fucking God himself.

Good God. So turgid, that last graph. Who really cares? When blunt existence whacks us out of reverie—when "reality bites"—we say, "I was disillusioned," as if illusion were good. College students look with trepidation on the "real" world and hope to remain in the delusions of higher education. Many in America favor "faith-based" initiatives over "reality-based" ones. Vacations are for "getting away from it all." To relax is to "unplug."

More, plastic surgery is now almost de rigueur, as are exaggerated Facebook identities, performance-enhancing drugs, genetically engineered foods. Cool, clean pixels trump steaming meat; gaming culture turns work to play; smarter computers will soon do our thinking for us.

We trust Jon Stewart, the host of a mock news show, more than the serious anchors of the big four networks. Millions of us follow Twitter accounts of television characters like Don Draper of *Mad Men* and Sue Sylvester of *Glee*, treating these phantoms as though they were real. One of our favorite pop music stars, Lady Gaga, is less an actual human than an ever-shifting pastiche of preexisting styles and performers—most notably Madonna, herself but an amalgamation of Lana Turner, Marilyn Monroe, and Marlene Dietrich.

At least we're getting rid of all that TV phoniness— canned sitcoms, sentimental family dramas, hyperbolic police procedurals—and replacing it with reality shows: *Duck Dynasty, Survivor, The Bachelor, Extreme Makeover, The Amazing Race, The Apprentice, The Biggest Loser, Queer Eye for the Straight Guy*, and *American Idol*. But the characters in these reality episodes are of course performing, even if unconsciously, because they know that their behaviors are on display to millions. And in falling into the stereotypes of TV Land, these "actors" follow loose, unwritten teleplays. Some cop good; others, evil. There are the cool ones and the losers, the zany neighbors and the overbearing bosses. The only reality these characters reflect is the fact that we're *all* characters in the massive reality show called life.

I am the Shalott Lady in reverse, sick of substance. Let's just go ahead and say it *is* all made up; then, at least if we don't like how things are, we can change the script, write a new, more pleasing plot, fashion the character we'd most like to be. And we might discover, strangely and paradoxically enough, that some fictions are truer than facts, and more revelatory, and beautiful, and good.

This vision is Lewis Carroll–surreal. To be a fake in this dreamy universe is to believe in actual authenticity and behave accordingly, and to be in tune with the real is to know it's all phony and to create, with a generous heart, your own sweet ruse.

4.

Prate about fakeness all you want. When you get liver cirrhosis, or Parkinson's or cancer, or watch those you love die in grim hospitals or hear of them getting killed on the highways or in war, then you'll look back on what you just wrote and feel shame. No veil can hide the skull.

Hans Holbein the Younger during the sixteenth century painted *The Ambassadors*. It hangs in London's National Gallery. To your left, if you're looking at this large painting (almost seven by seven) head-on, stands a robust ambassador, young and cocky, appareled in colorful finery, including a blue fur-lined overcoat and a salmon-ruddy silk shirt. He holds a fine golden dagger in his right hand. He is Jean de Dinteville, the French ambassador to Henry VIII. To the right is another French statesman, youthful as well, a bishop, Georges de Selve. Though his garb is more somber than Dinteville's, it is nonetheless as refined as Jean's, featuring a brown fur-lined robe, gracefully patterned. He is resting his left elbow on a book, which lies at the top of the two-tiered table between the men. Crowding the table are tokens of travel, knowledge, art, opulence—the best the world can offer. You see terrestrial and celestial globes, intricately painted, as well as a quadrant, a torquetum, and a sundial. A gorgeous Oriental rug, perhaps from Constantinople, an arabesque of rich reds, blues, golds, covers the table's upper part. Amid this rug and these technologies are books and a large, well-carved lute. Wholeness, twoness to unity gathered: Dinteville the secular hero, de Selve, the religious; heavenly globe and earthly; science and art; Occident as well as Orient. The universe, the painting pronounces, is harmonious, good, abundant, and Man, with all his implements for measuring and expressing the beneficent entirety, is at the center, the *best*. If you want Renaissance humanism in miniature, that period that produced Galileo and Shakespeare, Michelangelo and Vasco da Gama, here it is. What can man not make, from clothes to chartings stupendous, from stringed concords to godly thought systems? Nothing.

Nothing. But something's broken. One string on the lute. The harmony doesn't hold. And what's that gray-black creature-looking thing lying diagonally on the well-appointed Cosmati tile, arranged in the same pattern as the floor leading up to Westminster's high altar? Looks like a fish. No. More like an early draft for Ridley Scott's alien. Try to figure it out. Walk to the left. Nothing I recognize. To the right. That's it: anamorphism—a skull. Now anything's game. Scan all around the painting. Upper-left-hand corner, behind the hunter-green curtain that backgrounds these big boys: a small carved black crucifix.

This is a memento mori, "remember death." A synonym for it: a *vanitas*, all earthly striving, set beside death, which determines your soul's eternal reward or torment, is conceit alone, addiction to surface, triviality, nothing of worth. Labor for worldly success and its apparel: What's the point if you will soon come to naught but a worm comestible? In the corner of your resplendent wardrobe, there is a death's-head. Under the desk where you concoct your little treatises, you will find spines. Cultivate asparagus; bone fingers hide in the green. Chop a curving squash. It's a rib.

Jokes are everywhere, always on *you*. Hamlet humor: Great Alexander stops a barrel hole. Robert Herrick the jovial urges virgins to make much of time—diems to carpe, since that "same flower that smiles today / Tomorrow will be dying." Charlie Chaplin, Buster Keaton, the Samuel Beckett of *Godot*, and Lucky and Pozzo: all grace splatters in the pratfall, and in comes Albert Camus's Sisyphus, boulder-on-shoulder feeling, whose wicked grin does more than hint "I told you so, boys." Calliopes, yes, Bruce (kind of older), crash to the ground, and everything dies, baby, that's a fact, but everything that dies doesn't come back, no matter how fine the coif, the quality of cosmetics, or gambling on the Boardwalk. Alexander McQueen, to turn away now from the Boss, can weave all the skull scarves in the world, for Lindsay Lohan and Paris Hilton and the like, cracking campy on the vanity noggin, but poor man, poor boy, sweet, sad boy (no kidding here, none), hangs himself days after his mother dies, as mama-loving, easily, as too-too-sullied Hamlet himself.

I am a silly man, shallow, mocking most things, ironizing heaven and earth, desperate to escape the pain of time. But my mother got cancer, and my wit tripped. My father falls chronically ill: same. If my daughter were to come to harm, no way to fake it: I would be devastated, my laughter abysmally distant. Those chilblained medievals, for whom dirty, shriveled turnips were caviar, and fortune more fickle and blind than Sarah

Palin, were right: *Et in Arcadia ego*. Mr. Death is that annoying garden party guest, iron gate crasher, guy who won't fucking leave, and he is always a serious downer, but he'll also nag you into insight.

Death, sorrow, suffering, melancholia: all *real*. Blues music (Robert Johnson wounded): that's real. Elvis singing on Sun, '54, "Milkcow Blues Boogie"; that too, with its spooky yea-saying in the face of the inevitable earth's no-ness. What more? Dock Boggs's "Country Blues," back of Elvis's white trash transcendence, in which a dying gambler imagines himself as a corpse with its "pale face turned to the sun." Boggs is docked Keats-ward, though I know the banjo man doesn't know it, but: the bright face is brightest on the new corpse, or joy's hand is on its lips, bidding bye, and the pollen on which the bee sips, poison soon.

John Keats was the sometime friend of Percy Bysshe Shelley, killed in a boat wreck off Italy's coast, whose body was so putrefied when it washed to shore that it was unrecognizable, and identified only because on it was a copy of Keats's verse. Shelley never learned to swim, yet always teetered on watery edges, insisted on sailing, naked of life vest, if such even existed then.

Why so death-desirous, though healthy as LaLanne compared with consumptive Keats? Shelley saw in death the only truth, the one sure thing, bringing down colossal statues, Ramses-high-and-wide, as well as compact poets, like the five-foot Keats, whose hearts are nonetheless pyramid-dwarfing. Children grow up and away, ignore you, tolerate you, send you bogus greeting cards puffed with more sentimentality than the Lifetime Channel. Marriages, parting and dying, pass. Whole cultures crumble, and the noble tomes of Miltons.

Death does not. And sadness over these things fading drags you to death's door. Sit by it. A long time. It's all you've got. All I've got. To hold to. Handle. Ralph Waldo Emerson believed that "Even the corpse has its own beauty." He would know. A year and two months after his first wife, Ellen Tucker, died, like Keats (and Henry Thoreau and D. H. Lawrence), of tuberculosis, he walked out to Roxbury, Massachusetts, where she was buried, and opened her tomb, embodying by this gesture—not so strange in his day—his hunger for the truth. He had to see for himself his beloved's rotting body, the naked premonition of the only fact of his existence toward which he could safely express unwavering faith: his future was skull.

When I was twelve, I stood outside the varsity football team's locker room, and I heard one player, as he came through the door, say, "No practice tomorrow. Skull." He was talking to the player following him. Once in the open, they looked down at me, hesitated, and walked on. The one in front wore black horn-rimmed glasses and had long, bushy red hair, and the other sported a black T-shirt, tight over his gut, that said, in gold sequined letters, "Kansas." The skulls of my favorite tales, half buried on islands or decaying in caves, and this new kind of skull, connected with my dad the coach and his players, pulled apart my mind. My dad would soon emerge. He would tell me what this "skull" meant if I asked: a strategy session, attuned to the enemy's secrets. But on the drive home his steady talk about the upcoming game smoothed over the rift in my brain. I forgot to bring the subject up. It sank under my awareness.

The conjoining of football and bones didn't rise again until two years ago, when I was forty-five, and passed under the threshold to St. Olave Hart Street, one of the few remaining medieval churches in London. Sculpted into the gateway's arch are three grinning human skulls. Inscribed beneath them: "Death is light to me." I put it all together, as the hipbone is connected to the thighbone.

I want a skull of my own. Situate it on the surface of my writing desk, right there, just to the left of my computer. When I feel depressed or confused, phony or hypocritical, anxious, apathetic—anything but tractioned on this good green earth and as alive as milkweed—I will put my left hand on its smooth ivory-hued dome, and regain my grip.

"Yorick," I might intone, "alas, you are gone, and in your going, poor man, you remind me of what stays, which might be called: what I can't joke about, such as child death, wife death, death of mother, of father, of my boon companions—sublime interlocutors, training partners, colleagues I respect, literary friends, scholarly friends, friends, who, like me, give a shit only about twice a year, their soul's Christmas and Easter."

Such is the ubi sunt of memento mori, "ubi sunt" being another great conceit from the annals of literary history, meaning "where are," short for "Where are all the friends and treasures I once valued?" This is the sorrowful question of all elegies, those Anglo-Saxon ones in particular, "The Wanderer," "The Seafarer" ("No man at all going the earth's gait," so Ezra Pound's translation goes. "But age fares against him, his face paleth, / Grey-haired he groaneth"), each of which broods over what has passed, usually from a place of cold loneliness and starvation, in hopes, always, of discovering what does not go.

5.

In our materialist age, most of us, feet held to the fire, would claim that death, not God or soul or heaven, is the *realest* of the real. But every age has its vision of rock-solid reality, required, it would seem, for a society to function at all. We need a standard by which to measure truth, justice, beauty. Lacking it, culture turns relativist. Anything can mean anything, and paranoia begets anarchy.

Plato inaugurated Western philosophy by drawing a hard line between substance and shadow. He did so in a cave vision of his own, contra Herzog's. For Plato (called honey-tongued because bees settled on his lips when he slept as a babe), to gaze on gloomy shades dancing on a cavern wall isn't humanity's birth but hell.

Imagine men in a cave manacled so that their heads face the back wall. Behind them burns a fire. Between the fire and these inmates is a low partition. Other men move back and forth behind the screen, carrying statues just above its height: birds and fish, tigers and a bull, an athlete holding a discus, a girl with an urn. Those imprisoned can see only the shadows these forms cast on the surface toward which they, the captives, are turned.

On an unexpected day, one of these men goes free. Unaccustomed to light and objects, he is at first bewildered by the fire and the sculpted figures. Later, after he has sat by the flames and touched the shapes, he turns toward the cave's mouth. Curious over the even brighter sights beyond, he gropes toward the blinding sun. When he becomes used to the light, he ecstatically witnesses the living originals of the cavern's models.

Here Plato's allegory of the cave ends. The story demonstrates the philosopher's journey from appearance to reality—from the flitting shadows of uninformed opinion, to the more solid yet still ephemeral objects of the physical world, to the eternal forms: the unshakable realities (such as beauty, truth, and goodness) of which all temporal phenomena (a rose or triangle or a prayer) are but filmy copies.

(It is not surprising that Plato would locate reality beyond space and time, death and suffering. The bees lighted on his infant mouth as he slept in a myrtle bower on Mount Hymettus; he had been left there by his parents, who were sacrificing him to the Muses, just as Oedipus's parents left him in the hills to perish, for other reasons.)

Following Plato, Aristotle, Augustine, Aquinas, Descartes, Locke, Kant, and Hegel all labored to fix the real, prove that there is Being—stable, durable—against which to measure, and usually to criticize, Becoming—agitated ephemerality: alarm clocks, deadlines, grudges, confusion, indigestion, worry over children, pride in baubles, love unrequited, all things boring, baffling, exhausting, devastating.

I have read a lot of this philosophy, but I rarely can finish a chapter before I think of Plato's man who walked into the sun, of what he thought after he had been for some time in the glare.

Did he miss those dark days when all he did was watch shades dance upon a wall? He was then a constant spectator at a movie theater that never closed. Maybe he loved the illumined gloomy shadows, as a cinema aficionado would adore a weekend of noir. Perhaps these images were, despite their tenuousness, more valuable to him, more real and lasting, than the stable beings he now beheld. In fact, I imagine that he found his new home to be unreal itself, too tranquil and bright to be believed.

He sat down near a gigantic tree—not one kind or another—and ached. He wanted to go back to his chamber of peculiar illusions.

6.

If Plato were alive today, he would be Michael Pollan, and he would hanker for *real* food: tomatoes, apples, pomegranates, eggs, loins, flanks, arugula, red-skin potatoes, golden potatoes, blue potatoes, potatoes russet-colored, Cotton Candy corn, jicama, avocados, kiwis, pullets, ostriches, hogfish, sea bass, bluefish, red snapper, all the strange crabs you can eat, and mollusks (oysters and shrimp and such), navy beans, butter beans, collard greens, spinach, radicchio, fennel, leeks, bacon, sausage, pigs' feet pickled, and more tomatoes, those big bulbous ones, brain-size, German Johnsons, Better Boys, Cherokee Purple, Brandywine, and those smaller spheres, too, like fairy globes, the grapes, the Tommy Toes.

These foodstuffs unaltered would be to the latter-day Plato (now an ecologist), Being, as bright as the sun to a man emerging from a cave. Pollan is that man, because he knows the difference between real food and fake and worries that recent biotechnology is threatening the rich foodstuffs of our ancestors. In his 2006 *Omnivore's Dilemma*, Pollan reveals the ills of Monsanto, a corporate leader in genetic engineering. Monsanto has developed a genetic strain of potato, the New-Leaf Superior, which can produce its own insecticide. Its victim is the Colorado potato beetle, which can gobble in only hours all the leaves of a potato plant. But when this bug nibbles the NewLeaf, poison pulps its guts.

Upward of 395 million acres of farmland throughout the world are now producing genetically engineered crops, including, in addition to potatoes, corn, squash, soybeans, sugar beets, alfalfa, and papayas. Obviously, such alterations disrupt the earth's ecology. If you kill off the Colorado beetles, then you decrease the birds that eat such insects. What about the tinier bugs the Colorado beetle eats? If their predator is diminished, then will they overpopulate, perhaps eat other crops or weeds required for a given environment's thriving?

Ecological concerns aside, ontological ones press. Is a genetically engineered potato still a potato? Will humans soon replace naturally occurring DNA with artificial strains? Will the earth devolve into a true monoculture: man-made for the benefit of madmen?

These are apocalyptic questions and suggest that our sophisticated technologies are now pushing us into a crisis of Being more troubling than any time before. Not just biology is at stake; human consciousness is as well. This is what Nicholas Carr argues in *The Shallows*, from 2010. The World Wide Web, far from a utopian democratizing of education, is destroying our minds, not just by distracting us into quick, fragmented, surface bursts and busts of attention but also by altering the very neuronal structures of our brains.

I am more frenetic machine than measured man. I sit down to write, praying that I can sustain attention long enough to complete a paragraph. I compose half a sentence, type in a word or two that might push the thing to the finish, crave a break from the exhausting demands of syntax, *click-click*, and I'm at my home page, and I click my way to my e-mail. Maybe the editor says yes or there's an invitation from someone to contribute or lecture or just some person who loves my book and is writing to say so or maybe a friend asking for lunch, anything to tweak my ego, desperate-needy, or give me some-thing to think about other than that next phrase or clause, and as usual, nothing, not one goddamn thing. "Is my college's server down?" I wonder; "it's been thirty minutes since I've gotten an e-mail, for fuck's sake; surely the silence shouldn't be so long," and I soar, cursor-wise, up to bookmarks, go to sports-illustrated.com, must get the latest on LeBron James, same info as last time, ten minutes ago, and so click to Facebook, no message or friend request, so check out what George from my high school is doing, oh, having second cup of coffee, and now there's Valerie from the neighborhood posting another article on the mistreatment of otters (I just checked my e-mail right now, this minute, tenth time in past five minutes), and I've got to get back to the writing, but one more—*click-click*—over the *New York Times* page. Any book news? No, so why not check Amazon.com rankings for my most commercially successful book, no change, still at god-awful 510,357, but maybe there's mention of me on the net, a new review or blog praise, and so I Google my own name, nothing new, and then I Google my most recent book title, nothing new, and then I search my manic brain for any speck of curiosity that might take me to Wikipedia, still stalling, still staying away from the page of writing, and I think, Yes! Richard Hell, early punk pioneer, leadman of Voidoids, about whom I learned during a visit to

New York City, during which I sniffed the Gowanus Canal, and so I look him up, skim the entry, consider buying his recent memoir *I Dreamed I Was a Very Clean Tramp*, struggle to get my Nook to connect to my university's Internet system (I'm in my office), skim a sample, find it kind of sucks, check e-mail again (I checked it just now), remember—*I'm writing a sentence*—and return to that half-finished thought without an inkling of what the hell I was trying to say in the first place and so read back over the past paragraph, think, "Oh, yes, that's it," and scroll back to the fragment, and it comes, and I write it, and the sentence is decent maybe, and I start another, but wait, maybe something came on the e-mail, I'm not a bad writer, after all, so surely some editor is there, saying, yes, yes, and *click-click*: no, and so on.

Thus addled, and unable to control the crazed clicking, I, like Carr, have a funny feeling that an alien force has rewired my brain. What has happened is that my mind is becoming what it gazes upon: rapid flashings on a fragmented screen. The medium, as Marshall McLuhan said, before he played himself in *Annie Hall*, is the message. The machine makes the man.

(The results aren't always negative. For example, Nietzsche, who went mad when he saw a horse whipped. In 1882, he purchased a primitive typewriter, the Malling-Hansen writing ball. His fading eyesight—likely a result of syphilis—was making writing almost impossible. He could barely see the words he formed on the fading page, and the strain when he tried gave him terrible headaches. The typewriter saved him and invigorated his genius. According to a companion, the mechanism tightened Nietzsche's already compact style into something more potent: staccato, cryptic, elliptical, dense, runic. The friend didn't marvel, since he, a composer, had already noted that the quality of his "'thoughts' in music and language often depend on the quality of pen and paper.")

Generally, the mind on machine is dead: predictable, repetitive, numb. And the mechanisms grow more invasive. Google Glass will lock a screen centimeters from your eyes. Soon the chip will lodge in the cerebrum and control the yucky, squishy, prolix, slow, doubting, confused (imaginative, unpredictable, sublime) *brain*.

7.

Truth be told, though, you can't live every minute fearing that you're on the verge of turning robot, or straining for Plato's eternity beyond death, or contemplating a skull on your lap, living each minute as if it were your human last. Let's face it, if you were to do this, you wouldn't really be embracing instants to the fullest, whiffing roses and such. You'd be running from room to room, screaming, "I'm going to fucking die!"

There is certainly a time for remembering the grim reaper and cultivating the anxious intensity that might result. There's a time for forgetting, too, living as if you had all the time in the world to be your soft self casually, passing the time with movies or near-idle hobbies and the patient charms of art. Sometimes, as when you're laboring to publish a book, you have to ignore how difficult it all is, the odds of dissatisfaction or outright failure.

Cognitively, this overlooking is euphemistic, and it is a habit of mind I was cultivating before I knew nary a Greco-Latin polysyllable, as far back as kindergarten, the year before I learned my first word was "ball."

Imagine Ben Franklin wearing a curly shoulder-length auburn wig. Take away Ben's rounded Lennon spectacles, and put on emerald-green cat's-eye horn-rims attached to a silvery chain, and you have what Mrs. Goforth, my kindergarten teacher, looked like from ten yards away.

Walk closer, take in her powder-blue poly suit and almost same-color bluish blouse underneath, and then glance down, wondering what the hell kind of shoes this woman could be wearing with this monochrome habiliment. You see greenish blue open-toed boudoir-type slippers, covering panty-hosed toes. Stop three feet short of her, just out of bad-breath range, and a fortyish lady is there: moderate makeup, blue eye shadow (it's 1972), and wagon-red lipstick. She's not plump but a little beefy.

Mrs. Goforth is aware of her minor girth. Already twice she has absentmindedly half closed her suit jacket, as though to cover an imaginary gut. You don't think "big woman," though; she's about five feet six. Nor do you think "doughty" or "dull." Her posture is good, body seemingly alert, and eyes what we call intelligent, which really means that they're capable of staring without looking glazed and of scanning without appearing jumpy. She *is* in fact intelligent, this Mrs. Goforth, the mayor's wife.

Her face is now about three inches from my very own five-year-old face. She's not wearing her glasses, and she's staring right at my nose, which is bleeding. She's removing the packing, as she calls it, a wadded-up glob of those rough brown paper towels you find only in schools. I can feel the glob sliding out of my nose and can imagine that mixture of blood and snot trailing from it. She has the good taste not to show it to me, though I'd actually like to see it. I guess she has it in one of her hands. The other hand she's valiantly holding under the wounded nostril, in the cup form you'd use to catch spit-out gum. She wants to keep the blood, if there is any more, from dripping onto my already bloodied white shirt or the earwax-yellow linoleum floor. None flows, and so it all seems to be okay. I can go back to my table and cut construction paper and slop some of that good-smelling mucilage on it, making a Thanksgiving turkey.

I don't have a cold. The air isn't dusty. But the sneeze comes screaming down from just inside the high point on the bridge of my nose. I don't think to hold it in. A-CHOO!

This is before paintball, but it looks as if I had just shot Mrs. Goforth in the face, point-blank, with a paintball containing the exact color of blood or with blood.

She says, "Is there blood on Mrs. Goforth?"

"The red matches your lipstick."

Which it didn't in the least.

"Sweet boy. You'll go far in life."

8.

Did I lie to Mrs. Goforth? Or did I tell a "harmless untruth," a statement that falls between lie—intended to deceive, and so, contra the conscience—and untruth—saying something false without knowing it's false? (This nice distinction between lie and untruth is Montaigne's.) In his novel *Cat's Cradle*, Kurt Vonnegut calls harmless untruth foma, the essential idea of Bokononism, a religion composed solely of lies, but lies that "make you brave and kind and healthy and happy." Vonnegut seemingly intends Bokononism to satirize *real* religion, suggesting that it, too, is a system of lies that we believe in so that we can feel better.

Foma. That's what I laid on Mrs. Goforth. The white lie abuts this category: knowingly mixing the untrue with the true (perceived) in a way that generally isn't harmful and is sometimes helpful.

One of my babysitters, Wendy, upright and Christian, was, out of affection for me, a practitioner of the fib *blanc*. When I was ten, a boy whom I loathed, name of Dwayne, knocked on the door. Before Wendy could open it, I saw who it was through the window. I whispered, "I don't wanna play with him."

She said, "Go out on the back deck," reasoning that if I were on the deck, I would not be *in* the house and so, in a way, not at home.

I did, and she told poor Dwayne, "Eric's not home right now," and he left.

There are white lies, and then there are superfluous lies, serving no purpose other than to be *lies*. Remember Holden Caulfield, Salinger's hero who revels in this sort of fibbing: "I'm the most terrific liar you ever saw in your life. It's awful. If I'm on my way to the store to buy a magazine, even, and somebody asks me where I'm going, I'm liable to say I'm going to the opera. It's terrible." Throughout *The Catcher in the Rye*, Holden often lies for no reason, telling complete strangers made-up details about his life that serve no other purpose than to deceive people who have no stake in the deception.

I do it, too.

"Hey man, you run today?" a close friend asks.

"Yep," I reply.

"How far?"

"About six and a half miles."

"Cool."

I really ran eight.

"Hey man, what'd you have for breakfast?"

"Bagel."

Granola.

"Hey man, what'd you do last night?"

"I don't know. Just hung out."

Drank two martinis, a beer, a glass of wine, watched *The*

Awful Truth for like the five hundredth time, called police on loud renters in house next door.

T. S. Eliot wrote: "human kind / Cannot bear very much reality." I can't, reality being *what you can't do*, or the fall, as in "of mankind," which imposes—I'm treating the myth as true here just to make a point—one limit after another on all of us dwelling to Eden's east, ranging from gravity, to the necessity of getting a job for which you don't get paid what you deserve, to having to consume prunes in the morning, to death. To the earth's locked-in no-ness, the lie, gratuitous or not, asserts, "What*ever*," and conjures the "yes, yes, yes!" that suits the present fancy, and in so doing quests westward, hoping to sneak by the covering cherubs and reenter the Garden, where possibility burgeons beyond time and space. Holden and Wilson crave innocence: living in potential, eluding the actual. You might grow up to be anything when you're still unspoiled: tinker, tailor, soldier, professor. I *have* grown up, I am heavy corrupted, and I am a fucking English professor.

But maybe I don't lie gratuitously in a quest for innocence. Perhaps I do it because I do find myself, and life, boring, boring, boring, one trillion channels and nothing on, and I'll do most anything to distract myself just a little bit, to surprise myself, with the pitiful drama of . . . *what deceit will I blurt next?*

White lies, gratuitous lies. And then lies sinister. Deliberate put-ons that either harm others or help you or both together. Now we intrude into the lurid: cheating, stealing, swindling, conning, killing. I, as Poe's protagonist in "Ligeia," poison my wife, Rowena, while I sit by her sickbed, imbibing laudanum. I try to convince myself that I didn't do it, that the drug did. I lie to the constables outright, claiming that she died of a mysterious illness, knowing that, this being the early nineteenth century, forensic medicine, if such a thing even exists, has no way of proving otherwise.

I've mentioned only three kinds of lying. I've done all three. There are so many more types, more than I imagined. Go to Wikipedia, check out "Lie." Find "bad faith," or "lying to oneself" (Sartrean): "failing to acknowledge one's own ability to act and determine one's possibilities, falling back on the determinations of the various historical and current totalisations [*sic*, for an American] which have produced one as if they relieved one of one's freedom to do so." Bluffing, "to pretend to have a capability or intention" you really don't. Bullshitting, pretending to know much more about something than you really do. Emergency lie, employed to protect "a third party." Haystack answer: when you plant a lie amid other truths. Jocose lie, for comedy. Lie to children: "euphemism" land, or toeing tooth-fairy-might-exist line. Puffery. Bold-faced lie. Noble lie. Perjury. "View from Nowhere." Half-truth. And the Big Lie, one so extreme that no one would believe that anyone would have the gall to state it if it weren't true.

9.

Lies, of course, even the whitest of ones, require agency, a choice to fib or not. Moreover, a lie necessarily presupposes some agreed-upon standard of truth: what constitutes legitimate evidence in a court case, for instance, or valid testimony, or what proves a scientific hypothesis or constitutes fraud. In this way, lies are strangely reassuring, confirming as they do both free will and the reality they violate.

What is terrifying, however, is the possibility that both truth and lie are arbitrary antinomies—as are good and evil, rebellion and conformity, even, strange to say, life and death—in the collective narrative we have chosen to call reality.

Recently, sick and tired of my "death is life" dog and pony show—I've carved out about four books with that old saw (to change the metaphor abruptly)—and weary also of the melancholy literature I obsessively read (Lord Byron, W. G. Sebald, Thomas Bernhard), I fell into a period of reading Greil Marcus, the great psychologist of rock 'n' roll. I first read his *Invisible Republic* (also titled *The Old, Weird America*), in which he describes how Bob Dylan and The Band channeled in their

Basement Tapes the macabre deadpan lyricism of old-time Appalachian mountain singers like Dock Boggs (aforementioned), Buell Kazee, and Clarence Ashley. The book is powerful and nervy. "There's weather—the ordinary, the everyday, dirt kicked up by wind, a joke that leaves everyone gasping for breath, ten nights in a barroom and the boredom of waiting around for something to change—in the basement recordings most suffused with Judgment Day, and there is Judgment Day—a sense of visitation, the smell of fear, the appearance of the unwanted, ten nights in a barroom and the thrill of waiting for the end of the world—in the most weather-bound."

I thought: "Why the hell am I not reading Greil Marcus all the time?" And so I read *Mystery Train*, on the origins of rock 'n' roll, with a wondrous final chapter on Elvis, titled "Presliad," where Marcus describes the Sun recordings of '54, focusing on the "Milkcow Blues Boogie." Then I studied Marcus's *Lipstick Traces*, a history of the iconoclasm of the UK punk movement. In describing how the Sex Pistols created a record that changed the world by making "a breach in the pop milieu," Marcus recalls that old standby of sixties, seventies, and eighties French literary theory, championed by Jacques Lacan, Roland Barthes, Jacques Derrida, Michel Foucault, Jean Baudrillard, and Louis Althusser: "received cultural assumptions are hegemonic propositions about the way the world is supposed to work—ideological constructs perceived and experienced as natural facts."

For these French theorists, all so-called realities are actually signs in a ubiquitous, arbitrary language system into which we are born and that therefore "always already" shapes how we think, feel, and perceive. Inscribed in this vast volume are the primary values of the culture the words perpetuate. Generally, and sadly, these are the values of those in power, the 1 percent, and therefore rarely equitable. Hence our constant struggle against the sexist, classist, and racist biases embedded in our speech. (Remember the scene in Spike Lee's *Malcolm X* when Malcolm looks up the word "black" in the dictionary and finds all those negative meanings?) Even our "common sense" is a construct imbued with the assumptions, often unconscious, of the ideologies ruling our historical moment. And it's not as if we can rebel against these ideologies. They are so thoroughly embedded in how we think and speak that we can't get outside them, much less oppose them. And if we could rebel, we couldn't, since we possess no self we can rouse to revolt; we are but sites through which the master text works its way. No individual, no authorship of books, paintings, movies, music. This is what Barthes says. Herman Melville, Virginia Woolf, Jackson Pollock, Greil Marcus, Eric G. Wilson: all of us are simply exponents of the discourse universe into which we have been hurled.

(In 1980, Althusser, afflicted with a severe form of bipolar disorder, was massaging his wife Hélène's neck. Next thing he knew, he had strangled her to death. He alleged that he had no memory of the crime. The French legal system deemed him unfit to stand trial. After being confined for three years in an insane asylum, he was released. He wrote about his wife's murder in a memoir, *The Future Lasts Forever.*)

Marcus, optimistic, thinks we *can* break out of language's prison, that the cacophonous eruptions of Johnny Rotten and Elvis's Sun studio *wellllll*'s are creative, opening us to something contingent, unpredictable, mysterious, alive.

But most writers steeped in French theory, and not nearly

as schooled in Elvis or Rotten, or Robbie Robertson or Sly Stone, believe there is no escape.

Let's take an example of how "common sense" infects our *ways of seeing*, to italicize the phrase that is also the title of the 1975 book from which I'm going to borrow my illustration, by John Berger, the British essayist and novelist, Marxist in mood, heavy influence, as well, on Geoff Dyer, the great Montaignean essayist of our time, whose *Out of Sheer Rage*, a book about D. H. Lawrence, about Dyer's inability to write a book on D. H. Lawrence, turned me into a Dyer wannabe; he is so witty, honest, idiosyncratic, obsessive, petulant, weak, distracted, brilliant, insightful, lyrical, heroic. ("According to Huxley, Lawrence knew how to do nothing. He could just sit and be perfectly content. Not like me. I am always on the edge of what I am doing. I do everything badly, sloppily, to get it over with so that I can get on to the next thing that I will do badly and sloppily so that I can then do nothing—which I do anxiously, distractedly, wondering all the time if there isn't something else I should be getting on with.")

An image is "man-made," Berger asserts, and so is different from a fleeting visual perception. When an "image is presented as a work of art," he argues, the "way people look at it is affected by a whole series of learnt assumptions about art," concerning beauty, truth, genius, and so on. For Berger, these assumptions are often taken as reality, or "common sense." He calls this mistake mystification.

In 1664, the Dutch painter Frans Hals was over eighty and destitute. If it hadn't been for the charity of the local public administrators, who gave him three loads of peat to burn, he would have frozen to death. These same administrators commissioned him the same year to paint their portraits. He produced two, one of the regents of the old men's almshouse, another of the regentesses. The expressions on some of the subjects are striking, strange. One woman stares straight ahead, bitterly, judgmentally. Another's head is tilted to the right (her left); the half of her visage not covered in shadow looks askance at the viewer, as though she were a little surprised at what she's seeing, befuddled maybe, but no, it now seems that she's not confused in the least but has seen this all too many times and is tired of it, and can hope only for the third-rate solace of resignation. Of the men, one looks melancholy and drunk. His hat is not on straight; his hair is unkempt; one of his eyes is half closed, and the other, unfocused.

Most viewers of the painting, critics, art historians, and otherwise, have assumed that Hals in this painting set out to reveal the complexity of the human condition, fusing particular with general, dark with light, surface and depth, realism and allegory. Such interpretations grow from a basic cultural assumption about what great art does: it depicts with compelling accuracy feelings and thoughts that have universally troubled and enlivened the human race. Other assumptions underlie this one: there is a shared reality that the painter represents; some representations of this reality are truer, more beautiful, and better than others; there is something called *the human* that we all share. But these assumptions, which we take for common sense, obscure, Berger believes, the "drama of these paintings": between the gaze of the public officials and that of the "destitute older painter," who examines these officials "through the eyes of a pauper who must nevertheless try to be objective, i.e., must try to surmount the way he sees as a pauper."

In addition to obscuring this more interesting—for

Berger—drama, these commonsense assumptions reinforce the political status quo, implying that the current power structure is an expression of reality, not a construct that can be destroyed. And a main feature of this business-as-usual scenario is capitalism: superior works of art—the most real, the most beautiful, the most universal—are the most expensive ones.

If we accept these assumptions as self-evident reality, we don't exercise our ability to shape experience. We forget that powerful art, if we approach it without mystification, can, no matter its market price, grant us "the experience of seeking to give meaning to our lives, of trying to understand the history of which we can become active agents." To remember our agency is essential, unless we are to remain nothing more than quantified bits in a world of quantified bits, a world that has been reduced to commodity, where value originates not in intrinsic worth, in qualities like bravery, diligence, skill, prudence, compassion, but rather in how much something costs.

Of course, who's to say if Berger's account of the real isn't an ideologically driven interpretation as well? But if Berger's interpretation *is* ideologically driven, I *want* that ideology, since it empowers Berger to make this and other compelling claims that *open* possibilities for creative, invigorating, democratic interpretation.

10.

From the mid-nineteenth century up until the present, several capitalistic factors have duped us into chopping our lives into work, home, leisure. We put in our five hard days of labor so we can consume the delights of capitalistic economy come the weekend. And what does this leisure do but generate the desire for even greater leisure? And so it motivates us to work even harder. Home is between work and leisure. It is where we return after work to recover our energy for more work or more leisure. Ideally, as capitalistic units, we would do away with home time and buy into a cycle of work and leisure, since home, in this model, is rather unproductive and tedious, lacking the drama of building up capital to be blown on pleasure. Note how we attempt to turn home into leisure—"Let's not talk but watch TV or surf the Web"—or work: "I need to go to bed early so I can work harder tomorrow."

One can imagine a life, perhaps occurring in a preindustrial world, in which these three categories are melded, where one's work is an enjoyable craft that is an integral part of one's family life. But this life is no more—if it ever existed. Now it can only be *performed*, like a historical reenactment. In our culture of capitalism, mass media, and governments endorsing both, all actions, no matter how seemingly authentic, have been reduced to "spectacle," Guy Debord's term, which he develops in *The Society of the Spectacle*, published in 1967 and a powerful influence on the student uprisings in Paris in May of 1968.

Here's how that book, more pertinent now than then, opens: "In societies where modern conditions of production prevail, all life presents as an immense accumulation of *spectacles*. Everything that was directly lived has moved away into a representation." Life has declined from "being into having," a descent caused by the "total occupation of social life by the accumulated results of the economy," by the flattening of experience to consumption, quality to commodity. The next falling off, thanks to media saturation: from "having into *appearing*, from which all actual 'having' must draw its immediate prestige and its ultimate function." If what you have doesn't present you as what the media has deemed smart, sexy, intelligent, cool—doesn't cast you as a *celebrity*—then you lose value. Celebrities are the arbiters of value: "As specialists of apparent life, stars serve as superficial objects that people can identify with in order to compensate for the fragmented productive specialisations that they actually live."

My little life, awkward, insecure, sometimes hysterical, cowardly, occasionally graceful (blue-moon-rare), is nothing until I elevate it by witnessing a celebrity—"I went to the Springsteen concert"—or encountering one at close quarters—"and got his autograph"—or mimicking him accurately enough to where I take on his qualities but not so precisely as to be obvious in my imitation: "You were at that show! You got his autograph! Dude, that's the coolest. Let's go hang out." Success: I have turned into the commodity of my dreams: both a thing (a ticket buyer, a cheerer, a public booster) to make my favored celebrity more famous and a thing made more famous by my favored celebrity.

"I'm not like that," you quickly say. "I rebel against the mainstream. I am not ruled by what money can buy. And no, I won't be so obvious as to don Birkenstocks to mark my rejection of materialism. I'll get some secondhands at the Goodwill."

But Debord knows that "dissatisfaction itself has become a commodity." Going indie or alt or grunge or punk or goth or Dumpster diver or freegan or locavore or soft Luddite or Williamsburg dude: these roles take their value from the mainstream they appear to counter, gaining their "coolness by not caring about coolness" by virtue of the "coolness that cares about coolness" against which they rebel. These contrarian movements reinforce the culture they wish to challenge.

11.

So I'm in New York City a few months back, giving a talk on the gothic at this weird and wonderful nineteenth-century sort of place called the Morbid Anatomy Library, near the putrid Gowanus Canal, and at a certain point, on the visit, I find myself in Bushwick, the newest neighborhood to morph into hip coolness, or to become a simulacrum of Williamsburg. Near the Jefferson Street stop on the L is a largely Puerto Rican and Dominican neighborhood. The evening is fine—mid-June, seventy-five and a clear, slight breeze—and families are sitting on the steps in front of their buildings. With seemingly jovial un-self-consciousness, they are laughing, telling stories, drinking Coronas, joshing with children. One woman is on the sidewalk grilling hamburgers and hot dogs. About fifteen children play giddily in the steady gush of a fire hydrant. This is a culture informed by decades, if not centuries, of convention, a true *form of life*, organic, you could say, since growing from within outward. A culture that a person, like me in an early-summer twilight mood, might call *real*.

But then, after I walk awhile, I discover myself on Moore

Street near the Morgan Avenue L stop, and suddenly no more ethnic families delighting in the Saturday night respite from weekly labor. Instead, twenty-something Caucasian hip-cools abound, surrounded by requisite vintage shops, slick bars, and coffeehouses, as well as locally sourced restaurants. I have walked onto a movie set, where everyone is following the same script. Here, in cool world, where it's *happening*, nothing *is* happening.

But the families are acting, too. The parents and children "feel" more real because of the cultural conventions I've inherited—which say that "less calculated" (apparently) means "more authentic"—but I can imagine other contexts in which the hipsters would appear more attuned to what appears to be the case: it's all artifice. If we all are performing anyway, it's more sincere to playact deliberately, choose to do the things your culture deems cool. (What's *un*cool, for sure, is my assuming that the ethnic Bushwick families are less self-aware than the hepcats. The assumption is unfair, narrow. I'm sorry now for bringing it up.)

Anyway, you could say, siding with the hipsters, that it is cool to be cool, admirable to perform self-consciously. But you would have to know what "cool" means. There's Miles Davis, *Birth of the Cool.* There's Fonzarelli's "Cool it!" And then what about Kurt Cobain, who would "Rather be dead than cool"? Here we have "cool" as intrinsically good, a sign of effortless, almost deadpan grace and beauty; as a style alone, campy, fun; and as phoniness, opposed to authenticity, too tawdry for panache.

What makes George Clooney cool is that he seems "real," relaxed, comfortable, not full of shit. But another part of his coolness is his awareness that his "cool" is not really authentic at all, but a role he plays, as Clark Gable and Cary Grant and Frank Sinatra played it before. Yet another element of Clooney's cool, of course, is that it *is* a total put-on and nothing more, an ordinary man's simply trying to act out a fairly cli-chéd script going all the way back to Lord Byron, the first prince of cool, a script that aggrandizes aloofness, mystery, insouciant eroticism, leanness, confidence, eyes that flash. Part of the issue is timing, too. When to try to be cool? If you're too idiosyncratic in your effort—too early—you'll just be weird. If you're too derivative—too late—you're a wannabe. If you are somewhere in between, people will say, "That's new," and "That's what I've been wanting to do for a long time."

12.

Baudrillard, a disciple of Debord's who got some cool cachet when his work was featured in *The Matrix*, opens his *Simulacra and Simulation* (the book appearing in the film) by quoting Jorge Luis Borges's one-paragraph tale "On Exactitude in Science."

In that Empire, the Art of Cartography attained such Perfection that the map of a single Province occupied the entirety of a City, and the map of the Empire, the entirety of a Province. In time, those Unconscionable Maps no longer satisfied, and the Cartographers Guilds struck a Map of the Empire whose size was that of the Empire, and which coincided point for point with it. The following Generations, who were not so fond of the Study of Cartography as their Forebears had been, saw that that vast Map was Useless, and not without some Pitilessness was it, that they delivered it up to the Inclemencies of Sun and Winters. In the Deserts of the West, still today, there are Tattered Ruins of that Map, inhabited by Animals and Beggars; in all the Land there is no other Relic of the Disciplines of Geography.

In attributing this parable to one Suarez Miranda, who allegedly published the work in 1658, Borges emphasizes the difference between representation and the real. Whether the author goes by Borges or Miranda, the name remains separate from the man, an arbitrary marker pointing to a complicated, ever-shifting being that it can never fully describe or accurately locate. Likewise, a map, no matter how precise, even if it is so precise that it is exactly the same size as the terrain it aspires to chart, can never be perfectly in sync with the geography it graphs. If the map becomes one with the land, it isn't a map any longer, since the distinction between map and territory disappears. As long as the map remains distinct from the land, it continues to be, indeed, a map, but one that is necessarily inaccurate, in the same way that a menu entry "hamburger" doesn't come close to conveying the full meaning of the beef between the buns or that a paper bill lacks the weight and gleam of actual gold bullion. For those generations following the great cartographers, the territory-size "map" is useless, since it isn't, properly speaking, a map at all, but simply the territory. These children with no respect for their elders let the chart fall into desuetude.

Baudrillard claims that Borges's fable, a "beautiful allegory of simulation," has "now come full circle for us, and possesses nothing but the discrete charm of second-order simulacra." For Baudrillard "abstraction is no longer that of the map, the double, the mirror, or the concept. Simulation is no longer that of a territory, a referential being, or a substance. It is the generation by models of the real without origin or reality, a hyperreal. The territory no longer precedes the map, nor does it survive it. It is nevertheless the map that precedes the territory—precession of simulacra—that engenders the territory, and if one must return to the fable, today it is the territory whose shreds slowly rot across the extent of the map . . . It is the real"—Baudrillard continues—"and not the map, whose vestiges persist here and there in the deserts that are no longer those of the Empire, but ours. *The desert of the real itself.*" (Laurence Fishburne's Morpheus turgidly renders this last, of course, in *The Matrix*. That Fishburne's Morpheus is now hawking Kia cars is either perfectly apt or perfectly ironic.)

13.

Here I am, entrapped, like you, in early-twenty-first-century capitalism. No way to break out. And to dream of a precapitalistic culture or a postcapitalistic one is not only idle—since I can't go backward and can't control forward—but also grounded in ignorance, because I can't know if the past was just as spectral as the present and if the future will be. Such escapist dreaming is also depressing, setting up an ungraspable ideal, one that is in fact performative itself, a scripted rebellion based on the perennial dream of a golden age.

Life hurts me, as it does you. Though my pains are minor, so ridiculously minor, trivial even, compared with those of millions of others whose torments include cancer, torture, war, child loss, abuse. I suffer from what the doctors call bipolar disorder and so careen between heart-killing depression and fevered mania. Together, these two poles, often at the same time—my condition is "mixed"—threaten my ability to love, create, care. Or is it my weakness, my failing of will, that endangers these lovely actions? Whether because of these symptoms of my disease or my own shortcomings—or a combination, more likely—I am a mediocre father, pretty poor husband, negligent son, and self-absorbed friend. I feel constant guilt over these flaws but do little to change myself. I simply complain. I complain, too, about my lack of compassion. I don't volunteer my time to help others. About all I can manage is voting. I'm resentful of others' successes. I am terrified of failure, greedy for attention. I worry all the time, obsessively, about something awful happening to my daughter or her growing cold toward me. I dread her leaving when the time comes.

Common sense tells me that this suffering is real. Common sense tells me that my mom's getting cancer was real and my concern for her was real. Common sense tells me that my father is becoming frail and that my sorrow over this decay is real.

But how do I know? Yes, hurt, physiological, psychological, happens. You can measure it. Yes, people get diseases and die. No question, these things occur. Wars, rapes, murders happen, as palpably as these plastic square keys push back against my tap-tapping fingers. The question is, though: How do these events become *real* to me, to you, worthy of attention, interpretable, significant?

The answer appears to be: only through capitalistic lens. Suffering in this ideological context is an obstacle against which I struggle, in hopes of prevailing, as a soldier would battle an enemy, a climber, that impossible peak. Overcoming a bout of suffering—with strength, will, courage—I build my character, become a better man, more savvy, and more powerful, too, because suffering, as we learn from the Greek tragedians and Job alike, breeds *wisdom*.

This narrative is Faustian. Knowledge leads to mastery,

technological mastery in particular, the goal of which is to transform the earth into power and pleasure, an immense commodity. In laboring to manage my suffering, through religion or philosophy or ten-step programs or doctor's orders or pharmaceuticals, I am performing this ur-story: a resilient subject fighting a threatening object, with the aim of appropriating the object, morphing it into my subject, as a chomping mouth masticates gristly morsels in preparation for digestion. I am transforming suffering into spectacle.

How, you ask, could suffering take any other form? It is almost impossible to imagine it otherwise, I admit, so stern and so deep-delved are the economic wires in our heads. But what if suffering weren't viewed as a violation of the status quo, a veering from what should properly exist, which is a trouble-free life, padded with commodities? What if suffering was instead envisioned as an inevitable element of existence, so pervasive as not often to be noticed, ubiquitous and in the background and as essential as breathing? Then the individual's struggle against personal torment would simply disappear. With no enemy, no battle; no battle, no heroism or failure, no meaningful narrative. But isn't this more accepting stance toward suffering a spectacle as well, the rendition of the stoical sage?

Death is also a commodity, a pleasure. It is now but a challenge we trust doctors will one day overcome. You drag your decaying, diseased carcass to the clinic. Inside, the walls, the floor, the tables, the coats, all white, white-world sheen enhanced by instruments of silver, spangling, as stars, the unsmudged atmosphere. The god of this bleached land, the whitest, cleanest being in the domain, is the doctor. "Remove," he calmly commands, "those color-stained clothes, and don this frock of papery white. There. Now. Breathe. You have death in your cells, yes. But I will beat it, Jesus-flog your flagging Laza-ruses. We shall overcome. Fight, dammit. Live!"

Maybe don't go to the clinic, and see death not as an oppo-nent but as the good, cool, musty night, sweet oblivion, or as the old, gaunt, quiet fellow, William Burroughs–looking, with his skeletal visage, gray suit threadbare and dirty, fedora crum-pled, grip patched here and there, kindly stopping for you. But you can't imagine this brand of death for long unless you are Emily Dickinson, for whom death did indeed gussy himself up and then made a courting call to her home, probably in no fringed surrey but a black coach-and-six. But this scene ap-pears in a shortish poem, and many people (not me) find the morbid Emily unacceptably creepy (forgetting her exuberant verses on birds and flowers and storms). The point is, it's al-most impossible for the lot of us to view death as anything other than the grim reaper, to be feared and fought. And even when we try to view our demise more positively, as the not unwelcome visit of the eccentric old man, we do so in direct opposition to the more traditional image of the Ghoul, and to rebel is to reinforce the validity of the enemy. Our rival's strength grows in proportion to our hatred of him. Killing negative death only makes him more alive, a gigantic and swift skeleton who can cover the expanse from Tunis to Kan-sas's Lawrence in one easy morning ride.

14.

Global capitalism might well enclose us in a self-contained system whose antinomies only appear to be substantially different but are actually just arbitrary terms that keep the drama moving. But capitalism is just one particular system that happens to transform the world into one vast commodity: a quantity, an abstraction, a phantom. Obviously, other ways of seeing preceded capitalism, and even now there are premodern cultures untouched by Adam Smith. In addition, one can imagine other systems, such as Marxism, that value objects for their intrinsic worth and thus might bring us closer to palpable reality.

What if, however, our very mental makeup, our cognitive equipment, entraps us, regardless of ideology or even language, in a prison of our own perceptions? In *Metahistory: The Historical Imagination in Nineteenth-Century Europe*, from 1973, Hayden White argues that the study of history is driven by a desire to organize what happened—rife with accident, contradiction, confusion, mystery—into a cogent, meaningful linear narrative that reinforces the historian's current idea of reality. White believes that one of four basic narrative forms organizes historical accounts: romance, tragedy, satire, comedy. Each bears a political ideology. Romance expresses anarchy; tragedy, radicalism; satire, the liberal sensibility; comedy, the conservative one.

(For White, intensely ethical [after discovering policemen going undercover as students to monitor professors at UCLA, he successfully sued the LAPD on behalf of the university in 1972], the recognition of the fictional nature of history writing is a positive, because the awareness can serve "as a potent antidote to the tendency of historians to become captive of ideological preconceptions which they do not recognize as such but honor as the 'correct' perception of 'the way things really are.' By drawing historiography nearer to its origins in literary sensibility, we should be able to identify the ideological, because it is the fictive element in our own discourse." Such "self-consciousness" of the artistry of our own historical discourse should encourage us to ask: What presuppositions are organizing my narrative? Are these presuppositions on the side of oppression or democracy? How can I change my narrative to one that urges justice? Behind these inquiries is the assumption that we are free to transform time's randomness into meaningful morality.)

Thomas Kuhn is to science what White is to history. In *The Structure of Scientific Revolutions*, Kuhn claims that the paradigms of different cultures fashion different objective "truths." Ptolemaic astronomers really *saw*, given the assumptions of their culture, a geocentric universe. They found what they were looking for. Then, as in any compelling narrative, in which an antagonist and a protagonist tussle, Copernicus countered old Ptolemy's spirit—the man had been dead for centuries—by asserting that the sun is in the center. Liking this idea, Galileo a little later scanned the heavens for the central sun, found it, and thus "proved" that Copernicus was "right." (However, Galileo, poor man, faced a Catholic Inquisition prepared to burn men alive for challenging the geocentric Christian orthodoxy. He went on trial for heresy, and wishing, understandably, to avoid the fate of Giordano Bruno, burned a decade or so earlier for maintaining that the universe is infinite—not contained within concentric spheres—he, Galileo, renounced his theory of a solar core and so also of a moving earth, even if under his breath, apparently, he whispered, just after his retraction, *Eppur, si muove*: "Still, it moves.")

Galileo was able to release into the world an elegant analogy. Contrary to medieval theologians who envisioned the universe as a vast book written by God, interpretable in the light of his other luminous tome, the Bible, Galileo announced that the universe is a massive mathematical treatise. Isaac Newton, a century later, agreed, and proceeded to describe the cosmos as a gathering of indestructible atoms moving in a void, by gravity pulled and pushed, behaving with gorgeous mathematical regularity, as would a machine. And so began the Enlightenment, an age in which men looked for cogs and levers and perceived levers and cogs.

Charles Darwin, wallowing in the exotic messiness of the Galápagos, retorted: the universe is composed not of mechanistic atoms but of random genetic strands accidentally blending in response to unpredictable, perpetually shifting environments. Behold now, chaos cohering into temporary orders, which dissolve into chaos again. Look at consciousness around this time, too—late 1800s, early 1900s—and you'll see the brain itself not as a rational contraption but as a globular foam jostling on an inscrutable sea, Freud's deep. And so on, history-of-science-wise. The point is not that there's no such thing as matter or natural law but that the material and its principals take the shape that we mentally impose upon them.

Michael Gazzaniga, a leading neuroscientist, has discovered the cognitive mechanism behind the meaning-making activities White and Kuhn describe. In one experiment, Gazzaniga showed a series of pictures to a split-brain patient—an epileptic whose nerves between left and right hemispheres have been surgically severed. (He focused on this patient because the poor man's right brain couldn't communicate with the left, and vice versa.) Gazzaniga presented to the right visual field an image of a chicken claw. The optic information ran to the left brain, responsible for reasoning and speech. To the left field, Gazzaniga showed a snow scene; these data rushed to the right brain, specializing in sensation, intuition. Gazzaniga then directed the patient to look at an array of pictures with each of his eyes and to pick those connected with the claw and the snow. With his left hand, controlled by the right brain, the patient chose a shovel, thinking of the snow; with his right, left brain–guided, he appropriately pointed to a chicken.

When asked why he had chosen the chicken, the man, activating his speech-producing left side, said that he had connected, obviously, the claw with the chicken. But when queried about the shovel, he stated, still stoked by his reasoning left side, that the shovel was connected to the chicken as well, since one requires such an implement to clean out the coop.

Gazzaniga explains: "Immediately, the left brain, observing the left hand's response without the knowledge of why it had picked that item, put it into a context that would explain it. It knew nothing about the snow scene, but it had to explain the shovel in front of his left hand. Well, chickens do make a mess, and you have to clean it up. Ah, that's it! Makes sense."

This is what the left brain in all of us automatically does: it forms causal explanations for the right brain's sensations, and always after the fact, engaging in the *post hoc, ergo propter hoc* in earnest. There is no conscious perception that isn't fallacious, and the fallaciousness is "fudging" (Gazzaniga's peachy mot): the left brain torques data into a "makes-sense story." Of course, if lefty were honest in the chicken claw, shovel, snow, guano experiment (a surrealist fantasia of sorts), he would have said that he didn't really know why righty chose the shovel. But the left-brain man can't stand not knowing, and will "confabulate" in the face of ignorance, "taking cues" from what he does know to piece together a cogent, meaningful, causal narrative.

Gazzaniga calls the left brain the interpreter because it "engages in the human tendency to find order in chaos, that tries to fit everything into a story and put it into a context. It seems driven to hypothesize about the structure of the world even in the face of evidence that no pattern exists."

15.

Charles Sanders Peirce, pronounced "purse," was an emphatic asshole: arrogant, deceptive, pretentious, insensitive, sullen. He was also a genius, as a mathematician, scientist, philosopher, and manic-depressive. He was, moreover, left-handed. Finally, brilliantly predicting Gazzaniga's split-brain theory by almost one hundred years, he hated his mind's side—the right, controlled by the left hand—which made him crazed.

Peirce was born in 1839, in Cambridge, Massachusetts. His father, Benjamin, was a famous mathematician at Harvard, a founder of the National Academy of Sciences, and an acquaintance of Abraham Lincoln's. (He appears in an 1863 painting with Honest Abe, along with Louis Agassiz, for whom Thoreau, at a dark period in his life, trapped, killed, and tagged green brownish Walden turtles.) Austere, pre-free-range, outtigering Amy Chua by thirty cubits, Father Peirce pushed Charles toward tortured geniusdom. He forced his boy, as did James Mill his son John Stuart Mill (before *that* scion was redeemed by Wordsworth), to outrageous feats of juvenile erudition. Goaded by Benjamin, Peirce taught himself to read and write when he was not long out of diapers. Soon after, Benjamin sharpened Charles's intellect by forcing him to play a complicated bridge game, called double dummy, from 10:00 p.m. until dawn, sternly correcting the boy's errors. He encouraged Charles to solve difficult word and number puzzles, master chess, make up card tricks, and cultivate his own code language. He also engaged Charles in games of sensual discrimination, inspiring the son later to hire a sommelier to instruct him in the intricacies of wine.

Charles responded favorably to his father's rigorous regime. By the age of eight he was studying chemistry. At eleven he wrote a history of the science, and one year later he built a lab for conducting his original experiments. The next year he mastered a sophisticated logic textbook, Richard Whatley's *Elements of Logic.* By the time he turned eighteen he was deep into the thickets of Kant's *Critique of Pure Reason.*

Though Benjamin strictly dictated Charles's education, he also inculcated independence in his boy, empowering Charles to think for himself. This freedom, while beneficial to philosophy, was detrimental to character: Charles grew into a rule scoffer, a troublemaker. He was a problem student, a womanizer, impetuous, hot-tempered. He had trouble holding down jobs, maintaining professional connections, committing to romantic relationships. By the end he had squandered all his gifts, spending his final years battling drug and alcohol addiction, starvation, creditors, lawmen, depression, scandal, ignominy.

His last scene is pure Foster Kane, another Charles. There Peirce is, at seventy-five, with his second wife, Juliette, at his side, the only one (save the philosopher William James) with the gumption, or foolishness, not to abandon him. He lies on dirty sheets in a squalid room in his once-fine Pennsylvania manor, Arisbe, nestled amid the two thousand acres on which the rash intellectual had squandered his inheritance.

Peirce attributed his sinister behavior to his unorthodox dexterity. He assumed that right-handed people, which then, as now, composed 90 percent of the population, are right-thinking, their behaviors dictated by the left side of the brain, in charge of reason and logic. Lefties, the extreme minority, are, he supposed, right brain–ruled, and so unreasonable, illogical, tending to be contrarian, not right in the head, outcasts, evil, true to etymology, "left" deriving from the Latin *sinister*, which also means "ill-omened."

Peirce tried to rectify what he perceived as his imbalance by learning to use his right hand as well as he could his left. He willed himself into ambidexterity, digit-wise, fingers as well as numbers. He learned to write out complex mathematical problems with his left hand, while simultaneously solving them with his right. But this virtuoso party trick did not grant Peirce equilibrium.

(I am a lefty. I have bipolar disorder. I have tried, and failed, to learn to write with my right hand. I for six months contemplated writing a biography of Peirce. I found him too difficult for my half-ass brain, opted to write instead on Coleridge, another probable manic-depressive, a definite drug addict, and a poet for whom phantoms, even those of his worst nightmares, were profoundly more beautiful, and compelling, than facts.)

16.

Before Peirce intuited Gazzaniga's primary claim, there was the eighteenth-century Scottish philosopher David Hume, who was one of the first thinkers to deny a unified, essential self. He believed that we are "nothing but a bundle or collection of different perceptions." With our memories and imaginations, we shape these perceptions into continuity—a consistent "Wilsonness"—and causality: I am the effect of first uttering "ball."

This is an early version of the narrative theory of self that Daniel Dennett developed in the 1980s, significantly in the essay "Why Everyone Is a Novelist." Dennett substantiated Hume's idea with neuroscience, demonstrating that the brain possesses no central cognitive unit but rather processes data in several regions. What gives our being a "center of gravity" is language, with which we construct a cogent "I," to which we attribute, as we would to a character in a novel, intention, agency, rationality. Inhabiting this "I," we can explain otherwise confusing experience. Of course the identity we construct is not a simple unity but a network of diverse narrative flows: my story of myself as a son, a spouse, a parent, a professor, a man who appears a certain way in the eyes of others, including parents, spouse, child, workmates, and so on. This is not to mention the "wordless" forces—like our genes and instincts—that we must also negotiate.

For Dennett the constructed self remains the center of these crisscrossing stories. Paul Ricoeur, however, believes that our narrative networks are too complicated for central command. In his work in the late eighties and early nineties, this French philosopher (he died in 2005) envisioned identity as a heterogeneous, ever-changing weave of interacting narratives, with no one story consistently organizing the others. The narrative I create to make sense of my experience is already too complex and expansive for me to control, since my circumstances are changing in ways I can't predict, as are the lives of the other characters (family, friends, colleagues), the settings in which I and these characters exist, my community, my country, my environment, my planet, and so on. But these aren't the only factors that keep my narrative mobile. I also appear as a character in the constantly morphing narratives of the others in my life, as well as in the similarly shifting stories of my larger cultural network, and my role in these narratives can change the way I explain myself to myself and others. And of course most, if not all, of these narratives—both the ones I produce and am produced by—are ambiguous, paradoxical, unpredictable. I am not an original book but an amalgamation of millions of textual scraps, each of which is always growing, contracting, hiding. I am also a squirmy, multilayered fragment in the collections that make up the identities of others.

We can despair over how overwhelming it all is, how little control we possess over the crazed and multitudinous strands weaving our being. Or we can view this sublime interplay of cultural signs as an ethical invitation. That's what Ricoeur does.

He thinks that some narratives are ethical, and some aren't. Unethical stories are those unresponsive to the heterogeneity of the network, while ethical ones are sensitive to as many strands as possible. To create a narrative of such rich variety is not only good; it is beautiful, as the novels of Woolf, Faulkner, Proust, and Joyce are: capacious, multiple, polyvocal, rhythmical, generous. The fading of fact into fiction generates an ethics that is aesthetic.

17.

Wonder what Crazy Peirce would say about what I did in the spring of '84? I was a junior in high school, and bored, and, as randomly as a cloud morphs very like a whale, dressed up, along with my friends Baxter and Otis, as a disco dancer, and drove to the sad mall in the next town over and pretended to be a boy from Ohio trapped in a time warp.

We each sneaked our dads' seventies threads—from backs of closets, attic corners, dark basements—piled them on the twin bed in Baxter's little brick club house, and went through them as we would a Goodwill bin. We mixed and matched, got great glam.

I donned my dad's powder blue poly leisure suit, which he wore seriously back in the day, like, to *church*. I accessorized with brown buckle shoes, a wide white belt, and a thirty-inch fake gold chain, links nickel size, that I had found in the bottom of my mom's jewelry box. Baxter scored a leisure shirt, aquamarine moons floating among azure waves, denim bells, and a brown leather blazer. Otis: don't fucking remember.

We take the thirty-minute drive in Baxter's car, '67 turquoise

LTD. Otis soaks himself in Brut. Nausea rises up my gullet; I stick my head out the window. My Parker Stevenson coif doesn't blow around much.

We reach the mall. We prance down the dimly lighted promenade. High schoolers crowd the place. They gawk and giggle.

After a few turns, we settle near the decorative fountain, on a bench, side by side. Guys our age stand nearby. The largest of the bunch is paunchy, with a military do, dipping snuff. I recognize him. He is a linebacker on his high school's football team, which we beat three weeks ago. He doesn't recognize me.

"Where y'all boys from?"

"Ohio," I respond. "We're down visiting our great-aunt."

"We are brothers," Baxter adds. "Same mother, three different fathers."

"Shit," says linebacker's homuncular sidekick. "That's crazy."

Otis expands. "Yeah. My dad looks like Deney Terrio. His [pointing to Baxter] is more Adrian Zmed."

"What about him?" linebacker asks, pointing to me.

"Ever heard of David Naughton?"

"Who the hell?"

"You know, the show *Makin' It*. And *An American Werewolf in London*."

"Never heard of that. Why you boys dressed like that?"

"Like how? Everybody in our school dresses like this."

"Shit. You guys got football there?"

"No," says Otis. "I play badminton. Baxter, jai alai. Eric plays dodgeball. You don't believe us. We've got Baxter's cesta in the car."

Linebacker and toady and gang believe us. Seem to. They

leave. The three disco boys are left alone on the bench. We hear the grinding metal of the wire cages getting jerked down.

On the drive home we are silent. I look out the passenger window. The murk is not that now. The road signs are made of jagged wood. They point to Oz. When I get home, I return the clothes without being seen. A shower doesn't wash off the reek of the Brut. I imagine the lie I will tell my dad when he asks why I smell to high heaven.

18.

I had never done anything like the disco skit before and never did afterward, out of fear of looking foolish. But whatever motivated me that night, whatever muse or genie or cosmic dice roll, revealed the power of the swerve, the seemingly arbitrary wavering from the path, the more outrageous and unpredictable, the better, because abrupt breaks can't be righted; new direction is necessary.

Carl Solomon, Allen Ginsberg's friend, knew this. He once threw potato salad at lecturers on Dadaism at City College, New York. He wanted to *be* Dada, not just talk about it. Ginsberg reported the incident in "Howl," in which he blamed society for sending nonconformists like Solomon to "the granite steps of the madhouse with shaven heads and harlequin speech of suicide, demanding instantaneous lobotomy." Ginsberg first met Solomon at New Jersey's Greystone Park Psychiatric Hospital, where Carl was a patient and Allen was visiting his mother, Naomi, also an inmate. Allen was grateful for the erudite Solomon's talk on Dadaism. It soothed the traumatic event he recalled each time he crossed into Greystone:

the day when he as a boy admitted his terrifyingly paranoid mom and the gruesome return home: "12 riding the bus at nite thru New Jersey, have left Naomi to Parcae in Lakewood's / haunted house—left to my own fate bus—sunk in a seat—all violins broken—my heart / sore in my ribs—mind was empty— Would she were safe in her coffin—." When I read such lines, I am ashamed of so many things I have done.

The Dadaism Solomon enacted apparently originated in Zurich, at the Cabaret Voltaire, in 1916, when a group of European artists and poets disgusted by the First World War fortuitously stuck a knife into a German-French lexicon. The point penetrated the word *dada*, French for "hobbyhorse." Or maybe the movement grew out of the verbal tics of two Romanian artists, Tristan Tzara and Marcel Janco, fond of saying "da, da," meaning "yes, yes" in their native language. Another theory: "dada," like baby talk (such as "ball, ball"), is just a nonsense word to describe an artistic and literary movement devoted to nonsense.

If the culture responsible for the war valued reason, common sense, practicality, predictability, then to rebel required flaunting irrationality, nonsense, whimsy, accident. How best? Be Marcel Duchamp, the great hero of Dadaism, and create an artwork titled *Bottle Rack*. Around 1914, the artist bought the rack—designed to dry bottles, Christmas-tree-shaped, with metal spikes for branches—at a Paris department store called Bazar de l'Hôtel de Ville. It struck him as "readymade art," art simply art by nature of its existence, not because it was deliberately fashioned by an art maker. Duchamp had already experimented with such nonart art in *Bicycle Wheel*, a cycle's forked end and wheel mounted upside down on a stool. Unlike this work, *Bottle Rack* remained unaltered. It became art because Duchamp, viewed as an artist by his culture, called it art.

(Late in life, when Duchamp visited friends for the weekend, he brought no suitcase but rather simply wore the two shirts he would need and packed a toothbrush in the pocket of his jacket. If art is what you call it, so is packing.)

As lightning reminds us that electricity composes all matter, outrageousness reveals the normal. Finding a bottle-drying rack, calling it art, and people believing it's art, praising, studying, writing about it, calling it *brilliant*: this suggests that there's no such thing as ART—an essence, durable reality—but that we create the concept "art" and fit different happenings, some ostensibly reasonable, most simply *whim*, into this concept. Catapult a potato glob at a scholar and the splat echoes through the shocked audience, and everything, especially a serious lecture on a nonsensical movement, appears absurd. Go on an outlandish disco excursion in the middle of the Reagan eighties, and expand your mind to consider that perhaps even more serious identities, such as high school jock and big man on campus, are just as fanciful.

This is the assumption of Dada: the rules on which we tend to agree (beauty must be harmonious; knowledge must be objective and durable; identity requires stability) are fictions designed to comfort us in a world composed only of exceptions. That green-red flash in your eye's corner, that pitch in your ear, dog whistle–shrill, a quivery leafy splotch further in your periphery, in your gut queasiness recalling roller coasters: one impulse doesn't cause the other, but the blurs flit randomly and disparately, no logic, no repetition, until we blurt "hummingbird" and thus "noun" a world that verbs drive entirely.

Inspired by Dada, early surrealists also tried to shatter the nouns and return things to their silver eel mobileness. André Breton, one of the movement's founders, channeled the playful spirit of the nineteenth-century poet Comte de Lautréamont, who wrote of a certain young boy that he was "as beautiful as the chance encounter of an umbrella and a sewing machine on an operating table." For Breton, this line expresses the surrealistic ideal, occurring when the juxtaposition of "two distant realities" produces a novel third state. After emerging from a hypnogogic reverie, Breton discovered such a striking contiguity torqueing his head: "There is a man cut in two by the window." Gifts from the unconscious like these inspired Breton to believe that the mind is most creative when unhindered by reason as well as by aesthetic or ethical concerns. From dream, reverie, trance—states conductive of "psychic automatism"—arise the random effusions that make the greatest art. The most famous of the surrealists, Salvador Dalí, presented happenstance absurdities in painting after painting and also in the oneiric film he made with Luis Buñuel, *Un Chien Andalou*, which featured ants creeping out of a hand's skin and the eyeball of someone sliced open, and which also heavily influenced America's cinematic surrealist David Lynch, who entered the world's consciousness through a severed ear.

Debord, deep in surrealism and Dada, believed that we can destroy controlling narratives through "situations" that momentarily shut down predictable capitalistic perception, which reduces things to commodities, and expose us to fresh happenings. One such deliberate occurrence is the *dérive*, or "drift," in which a group or individual randomly draws a line on an urban map and then walks the line. No longer economically purposeful, the walk becomes that, a *walk*, an experience for the sake of experience, meaningful in ways not economically determined. Ideally, as Debord and his "situationist" colleagues put it in 1960, such situations would offer "moments of rupture, of acceleration, *revolutions in individual everyday life.*"

For Marcus, as I have hinted, certain moments in the history of rock 'n' roll—ranging from Harmonica Frank Floyd's "The Great Medical Menagerist" to Jonathan Richman's "Roadrunner"—are pure Dada. They are eruptions that can redeem us from the "politics of freeze-out" ruling almost any culture, which turn it into "seamless melancholy" that numbs people into a "willful avoidance of anything . . . [that] might produce really deep feeling." These startlingly dark-bright musical effusions are "so intense and compelling" that we will risk the chaos of feeling "to get close" to them, so potent that they smash "through a world that for all its desolation may be taking on too many of the comforts of familiarity."

19.

I had an encounter with Carl Solomon. It was the fall of 1991. I was taking a Ph.D. seminar on the Beat Generation taught by Ginsberg himself, who from time to time rolled out bygone Beats to guest lecture.

One day there was the toothless, crazed, and wild-haired Gregory Corso, drinking from a large glass bottle what had to be vodka mixed with orange juice. He reminisced fondly over his first meeting with Allen at the Village's Pony Stable and espoused, vehemently, his latest theory of cosmogenesis, based on his idea that somehow the universe began as a point, then evolved to a line and a plane, eventually blossomed into a rhombus, and finally expanded into a dodecahedron. Another day, accompanied by a beautiful twenty-something boy assistant, Herbert Huncke appeared. His junkie days had drained his brain of thought, affection, almost word. All he could do was continually contort his right hand into a claw, relax it, and do the same again.

Then Solomon came: a cross between Carl Reiner and Marvin Kaplan (the guy who played that telephone repairman in the TV show *Alice*). He wore a heavy beige coat, with a fur-lined hood, and large, thick glasses with squarish plastic frames. He was irascible, none too happy to be pulled out of whatever life he was conducting there in the city, and quite reluctant, understandably, to discuss his times in the asylums back in the forties and fifties, when he underwent brutal shock therapy treatments.

Realizing that his informal interview with Carl wasn't going too swimmingly, Allen asked him to read from his 1966 book *Mishaps, Perhaps*, which describes his stints in the psychiatric hospitals, focusing on the inhumanity of the treatment. Allen requested a passage satirizing the square American society of the day. Carl began to read quickly in this totally flat tone, no intonation here or there, barely a pause for period or comma, nothing emphasized over anything else. Far from comical, the performance was disturbingly weird and sad.

Allen grew increasingly irritated, every few sentences interjecting imperatives like "Slow down" and "Emphasize that more." Carl read as if Allen weren't even there. Finally, after about three minutes of this, Allen said, with resignation, "Okay, okay," and reached over and took the book from Carl's hand. Carl put his empty hands under the table, said nothing, and stared straight ahead as he might have on the subway on a late-night ride home. Allen then reread the passage. It was very funny.

This wasn't the first time Ginsberg behaved a bit brusquely. The first day of class, during a lecture on the literary influences on the Beat movement, he referred to Shelley's "Ode to the West Wind." He must have received some blank stares because he said, "Surely all of you have read this Shelley poem. Who in here hasn't?"

Only one student raised her hand: a tall, pale woman with close-cropped blond hair. She wore small, round glasses with thin silver-blue frames, and a black leather jacket.

Allen frowned. "What? You call yourself a Ph.D. student and haven't read the ode? That's shameful."

The woman—all of us at the seminar table had turned to watch her—blushed ferociously. Then she spoke in a slight German accent, gently, humbly, "I am German and have not had the same education in English literature. I will read this poem. Thank you for suggesting it."

Allen put his hands together as though he were praying, slowly closed his eyes, and slightly bowed, with the grace of a saint, her way.

But we graduate students, resentful, as are most graduate students in English, forgot this sweet gesture, an elegant harmony of apology and admiration, and instead focused on the earlier, more mean-spirited remark. We took to calling Ginsberg the Rude Buddha.

I'm now ashamed of myself for mocking Allen Ginsberg, who had such a capacious, tender, fierce, sorrowful, song-bursting heart and had simply wanted, in lifting the volume from Carl, to restore his first hero's language to its proper Dadaesque wit.

20.

Borges explores this Dadaist gap between constructed generalizations and ungraspable particulars in "Funes, the Memorious." Ireneo Funes is a boy from Uruguay who remembers everything in overwhelming detail. He cannot grasp why a "dog at three fourteen (seen from the side) should have the same name as the dog at three fifteen (seen from the front)." He is so attentive to particular moments that his "own face in the mirror, his own hands, surprised him every time he saw them." He "could continuously discern the tranquil advances of corruption, of decay, of fatigue. He noted the progress of death, of moisture. He was the solitary and lucid spectator of a multiform world which was instantaneously and almost intolerably exact." Even the "ferocious splendor" of Babylon, New York, London is pallid in comparison with the "heat and pressure" of Funes's recollections.

Funes staggers under these heavy details because he is "almost incapable of ideas of a general, Platonic sort." How, he asks, can "the generic symbol dog [embrace] so many individuals of diverse size and form?" He cannot think, if thinking "is to forget differences, generalize, make abstractions."

Funes could have been a great Dadaist, experiencing without effort the kind of buzzing rawness for which Duchamp, Solomon, and Wilson as faux Travolta strained. But the burdened Funes would actually have welcomed boring abstraction. Think of the peace of "Continuity," for instance. You get a sore throat. You're not worried, though. You've had one before, felt just like this one, and healed within five days. There's no reason, you conclude, that this one won't do the same, and you relax. What if you have no durable concepts of "sore throat," "past," or "healing"? Every new sore throat would be shocking, terrifying, as would every storm or death. These relentless startlings exhaust and sadden Funes. He dies sorrowful and young, of the "congestion of the lungs," killer, as we know, of so many hypersensitive souls, such as Keats.

The melancholy grandeur of Borges's "Funes" makes Dadaist shenanigans look rather silly, immature mocking of authority. Sure, authority for the rebel is a drag, but certainly some authority is necessary for a thriving existence, animated not only with continuity (we can cultivate values over time) but also with community (we can share similar values) and comprehension (we can understand what it means to love or to heal).

Still, I can see why Duchamp and Solomon were suspicious of authority, since most people in charge are, with varying degrees of awareness, oppressive, imposing their fantasies of power onto facts, laboring to blur the distinction between the two, hoping finally to force the multitudes to accept their fantasies as the only facts.

21.

Can there be a middle way between the systems loathed by the Dadaists and the "isness" exhausting Funes? If so, might this golden mean establish moral ground?

Immanuel Kant, the late-eighteenth-century philosopher from Königsberg, was famous for the regularity of his walks. The villagers set their clocks to his passing by. Perhaps Kant was strict in his strolling to balance his somnolence. According to an early-nineteenth-century English biographer, Thomas De Quincey (a notorious opium addict who wrote a memoir about his habit), Kant suffered from "unseasonable dozing" that caused him to fall "repeatedly, whilst reading, with his head into the candles; a cotton nightcap which he wore was instantly in a blaze, and flaming about his head." Kant, though, might have found the danger stimulating, for it was precisely a rude awakening from his "dogmatic slumbers" that inspired him to grapple brilliantly with the problem of whether we can access meaningful matter beyond our minds.

For the first half of his philosophical career, Kant was a rationalist in the tradition of Leibniz, Spinoza, and Christian von Wolff: he believed that rational inquiry revealed a rational universe. But then Kant read Hume, the Scottish empiricist who argued that if we gain knowledge only through sense experience, then we are able to perceive only sequence, not causality. The falling pocket watch is at this height one instant and another the next, and so on. We have no basis to conclude that gravity pushes the mechanism earthward. Kant reasoned: If Hume is correct, then a primary rationalist assumption—the universe functions according to strict cause and effect—is untenable. Not just that, science itself is worthless.

Burned awake, Kant devoted himself to saving causality and so, science. This redemption required a Copernican revolution—not for cosmos but mind. Kant agreed with Hume: we cannot perceive causality. But causality must exist somewhere; otherwise, all is chaos. If not in matter—at least in a way we can comprehend it—then why not in mind? Yes, causality—as well as quality, quantity, relation, and such—is *mental*. The mind regulates the raw data streaming into it, translating fluxes into pattern. But the true nature of a thing—the ding an sich, the "thing in itself"—remains mysterious. We can only understand the phenomenal realm—what presents itself to the mind's categories—never the noumenal: unmediated *thisness*.

This system—Kant developed it in his 1781 *Critique of Pure Reason*—works nicely for science, which focuses only on phenomena. What, though, of morality? According to Kant in his 1788 *Critique of Practical Reason*, morality requires noumena—freedom, God, and immortality: freedom as a basis for choosing between good and evil; God as a guarantee that we will be rewarded for choosing good; immortality as the realm where the reward is truly enjoyed. Obviously, we can't prove that such entities exist, as we can validate, say, gravity. But that doesn't mean they don't exist, nor does it—this lack of proof—preclude belief. If freedom, God, and immortality are necessary for moral behavior, then we must indeed behave as if they existed. Treating such concepts as real produces moral reality. The abstractions of the mind and matter's immediacy, the fake and fact, blend into a vision of each person's intrinsic worth.

22.

A disciple of Kant's, Arthur Schopenhauer strove to find the moral mean between our constructs and existence. He was also, like Kant, a habitual walker. Not, it appears, for his own exercise, but rather for the health of one of the many poodles he owned during his seventy-two years. He formally named each one Atma, suggesting *atman*, the Hindu term for the eternal soul animating all individuals; he called his pooches, though, the more affectionate Butz. Some believe that his calling his different poodles—he especially loved a white one and a brown one—the same name exemplified his idea that animals could express almost no individuality, that they were simply similar exponents of the species.

Humans, he believed, are more aware of the *principium individuationis*, the principle of individuality. This principle shows Schopenhauer at his most Kantian. Reality for him, as for Kant, is ultimately unknowable, a mysterious irrepressible, selfish, desperate will to life. This Will, Schopenhauer's version of the ding an sich, goads nature as well as humans to go to any length to survive, regardless of the welfare of others. Humans, however, at least struggle to understand the Will, and they do this by exercising their a priori cognitive power to individuate, to represent the unrepresentable Will to themselves in diversified spatial and temporal forms. Schopenhauer held that all human perception and knowledge are products of this mental mapping (akin to Kant's categorizing) and thus are, like maps, approximations of a territory they can never capture with total accuracy. Such is the primary argument of Schopenhauer's 1818 *The World as Will and Representation*.

Schopenhauer held that as long as we are controlled by Will, we are miserable, consumed with egotistical desires whose unfulfillment breeds pain and whose satiety causes boredom. We gain peace only by realizing that we and everyone else are driven to suffering by Will, and by consequently developing compassion for the collective. We all are in this together, so let's help one another out. Acting on this insight, we temporarily deny our Will, escape our selfish striving.

Another way we ease our pain is by contemplating great art. Engrossed in *Hamlet* or Caravaggio's *David*, we rise from our narrow "I" to contemplate, intensely, ecstatically, the universal. Of all the arts, music is the most powerful, since it transcends word and image and directly presents the oneness of the Will, and so transports us into an intuition of the unity behind diversity: "Music does not express this or that particular and definite joy, this or that sorrow, or pain, or horror, or delight, or merriment, or peace of mind; but joy, sorrow, pain, horror, delight, merriment, peace of mind themselves, to a certain extent in the abstract, their essential nature, without accessories, and therefore without their motives. Yet we completely understand them in this extracted quintessence."

23.

In October 1865, a twenty-one-year-old Nietzsche admitted that he didn't know "which demon" forced him hastily to buy Schopenhauer's *World as Will and Representation* at a second-hand bookshop in Leipzig, but he was glad of the imp, because as he read the volume after throwing himself into "the corner of the sofa," he "saw a mirror which caught sight of the world, of life, and of my own mind in terrifying grandeur." So began Nietzsche's lifelong struggle with the older philosopher, whom he initially worshipped, later reconsidered, and finally renounced. When he was still in his adoration stage, he subtly extended Schopenhauer's thought to Greek tragedy.

In *The Birth of Tragedy*, from 1872, Nietzsche asserted that the dramas of Aeschylus and Sophocles were art in its highest form because they achieved balance between the Dionysian—analogous to Schopenhauer's Will, nature in its horrific yet exhilarating indifference to human suffering—and the Apollonian, the forms, beautiful but limiting, that humans create to comfort themselves, close to Schopenhauer's realm of Representation. Whereas most artworks veer too far to one side or the other—toward unsettling chaos or stilted order—ancient Greek tragedy expresses Dionysian energy through the music of the chorus and Apollonian restraint via the dialogue's poetry. The content of the plays—how we find meaning in life's inevitable suffering—reinforces the form.

One year later Nietzsche, in an essay titled *On Truth and Lies in a Non-Moral Sense*, suggests that human knowledge is Apollonian—illusion—while reality is Dionysian, beyond word and image. What most consider truth, then, is "a mobile army of metaphors, metonyms, and anthropomorphisms—in short, a sum of human relations which have been enhanced, transposed, and embellished poetically and rhetorically, and which after long use seem firm, canonical, and obligatory to a people: truths are illusions about which one has forgotten that this is what they are; metaphors are worn out and without sensuous power; coins which have lost their pictures and now matter only as metal, no longer as coins."

The goal of the philosopher is not to try to break through Apollo to Dionysius. This is impossible. What he should do is aspire to Sophocles: become an artist. He should be aware that all knowledge is art already and that most of it, because dogmatically fixed on one metaphor to the exclusion of all others and interested only in perpetuating its principles, is bad art: limited, predictable, static. The thinker should use this consciousness as muse: to inspire him to create new knowledge, more capacious, spontaneous, dynamic.

24.

Nietzsche suggests a startling criterion for truth: those ideas that are true are not so because they correspond to fact but because they enrich life. Hans Vaihinger, a disciple of Kant, Schopenhauer, and Nietzsche, explores this notion in his delightfully titled *The Philosophy of "As If,"* completed in the 1880s, published in 1911. Like his teachers, Vaihinger maintains that we can never fully comprehend a reality composed of fleeting feelings and sensations. However, we nonetheless are constantly behaving as if our beliefs about reality were actually true. For instance, we cannot directly observe atoms, but only the field they produce. Still, we believe they exist and act accordingly, carrying out atom-based scientific projects that improve our lives. The same can be said of Kant's triumvirate, freedom, God, and immortality; to behave as if each existed can ameliorate self and other. Likewise continuity, the future, purpose: though we cannot in any present moment prove the reality of these, we require them to thrive. They are useful fictions.

Can we make up just any fiction we'd like and call it true?

No. Fictions must be "pragmatically justified" to be valid. If I think I can fly and so leap off a cliff and die, then my belief not only possesses no pragmatic use but is deadly. But if I maintain that my volunteering at a homeless shelter will merit reward in future—emotionally, psychologically, monetarily, or spiritually—and so volunteer and provide food and comfort for those that suffer, then my belief is useful for me and society. Likewise, belief in the electron can result in productive cancer research, cures for fatal viruses, our understanding of the origins and ends of the earth.

If we can't break through our fictions to knowable fact, we can at least fabricate facts through invigorating fictions. And these fictional facts can be as harmonious and beautiful as the suppleness of our feelings and sensations will allow.

25.

On July 1, 1985, I entered the United States Military Academy, West Point, as a prospective quarterback for Army's football team and as a new cadet. (I have told this story in print before, but from another angle, for another purpose, emphasizing different aspects. There might be some overlap in detail, though.) During the next days, I got a high-and-tight. I was hazed all to hell: berated, mocked, made to do hundreds of push-ups. I was awakened at daybreak by the squad leader clanging a baseball bat inside a metal trash can. I ran, crawled, did sit-ups, duck-walks, more push-ups. I memorized passages from *Bugle Notes* (a little gray anthology of army wisdom, such as "Schofield's Definition of Discipline": "He who feels the respect which is due to others cannot fail to inspire in them regard for himself, while he who feels, and hence manifests, disrespect toward others, especially his inferiors, cannot fail to inspire hatred against himself"). I memorized the number of days, shrinking, until Army would "beat the hell out of" Navy in the annual football game. (One prissy member of my squad initially refused to say "hell"; he said "heck"; the squad leader's verbal reaming still makes me feel naked, pale, and stupid.) Every day I memorized one front-page story and one sports story from *The New York Times*. I memorized the daily mess hall menu. When I forgot, and I did, upperclassmen screamed at me as if I'd broken a ball of ruby glass they'd blown themselves. I attended classes on "Duty," "Honor," and "Country." I participated in football meetings and workouts. Along with all the other new football players, I visited the head coach's house one Sunday. I ate a whole column of Oreos. I learned to fire an M-16. I learned to wield a bayonet, motivated by the constant catechism: "Upperclassman: 'What is the spirit of the bayonet?' New cadet: 'To kill, sir!'"

With my body—eighteen and strong and tough—I did all these things. But my mind, from the first five minutes I was there, whispered over and over, like a prayer, "Got to get the fuck out of here."

Why the violent aversion? That first day of Beast Barracks I saw writ large the values that had been pressed into me: aggression is good; violence is necessary; obey authority; be patriotic; discipline is essential; justice trumps mercy; short hair is better than long; pressed is superior to wrinkled; idleness is the root of evil; sincerity lords over irony; tragedy rises above the comic; Churchill is more heroic than Chaplin; the United States of America is the Greatest Nation on Earth.

As these doctrines slammed into my still uncalcified brain like Underwood keys the size of Thor's hammer, boldface, all caps, I felt in all my nerves, *NO*, the burn of negation, the *not*. I didn't know what I wanted, but I knew exactly what I *didn't want*. To salute the colonel. To say "Yes, sir." To aim straight, keep it in line, stay the course. To flag-wave. To shoot a man in the head.

I had to stay, though, at least thirty days, as did all new

cadets. My squad heard rumors of one boy's going AWOL into the Catskills. We heard of another who attempted to slit his wrists with a plastic butter knife. Too timid or prudent for such extremes, I decided to wait it out as best I could, as smoothly, so I told no one of my decision and tried to be a seriously squared-away new cadet.

The PT was no trouble, since I had been regularly running and lifting over the past several years. My recitation of the menu and the number of days to the Navy game and the definition of discipline: not so difficult either. Used to performing under pressure—leading the last-minute touchdown drive—I could remain calm when quizzed. Guys much smarter than I—scary-high SAT scores—broke down.

My problem was sleep. Though my ache to resign never lessened, I was still anxious, mainly over how my dad would react. A fanatical Vince Lombardi disciple—"Winners never quit and quitters never win"—he would be disappointed over my dropping out. My squandering a good opportunity to play college football would also hurt him. I was also embarrassed. I was my high school's and community's first ever West Pointer, and everyone who could read a local paper knew it, and I was now dragging my ass home, a failure.

But there was deeper unease. If no longer Wilson the athlete, the fine young man, the favorite son, the golden boy, the youth of great promise, the big fish in the little pond, now swimming to sea, then who, now, was I?

The question wasn't this simple. The break didn't need to be so sharp. I could certainly remain all these things, but in another context—another college, for instance, smaller probably. I could try out for a team, win a scholarship, turn it all around.

But I craved clarity, a clean severing: to cut the cloth, weave anew, leave Achilles for Hamlet, the action man for the contemplative, concussion for consciousness.

What could soothe, at night, my exhilaration and fear?

I had brought one book with me to West Point. It was a whim. The day before I left, when out buying toiletries I would need on my trip, my mom passed the pharmacy's mass-market paperback rack and thought that she might buy me a book to cheer me up during basic training. She studied the titles until she happened upon a book on whose cover was Bill Murray, my favorite actor. He was standing in front of an old temple high in a mountain range, wearing a burgundy sarilike wrap over a rough woolen shirt striped white, yellow, and bright red, with a lapel the same burgundy as the wrap. He gazed contemplatively into the distance, head tilted slightly upward. The title of the book was *The Razor's Edge*. In a hurry, my mom didn't bother to read the back cover or the first few pages. She just assumed that the volume was either about Murray or by him, not realizing that Murray was playing in a film version of this novel by W. Somerset Maugham. The book's cover was the movie tie-in.

Busy, anxious, I barely noticed the book I found in the shopping bag my mom handed me, but just threw it into my suitcase along with the deodorant, toothpaste, and shaving cream. Later that day, when Mom mentioned that she had bought me a book about Bill Murray, I said, "Yeah, I saw it, packed it, thanks," and then I pretty much forgot the whole thing until I came across the book while unpacking the next day, my first at West Point. Reading was far from my mind just then. I put the volume in a desk drawer in my barracks.

But as I was lying awake on the third night after my arrival, trying to slow my mind's whirligig, I thought that reading might calm me. I retrieved the book, returned to my bunk. How would I read it? I couldn't turn on the light; in the military, "lights out" means "lights the fuck out!" But there was a moony glimmer in the window beside my top bunk, in whose grayness I could discern faintly the script, as though it were submerged in a mud puddle, but not enough to read without getting a headache. I then tried the light on my Casio wristwatch: just enough, when compounded with the lunar glow, by which to read the first sentence, "I have never begun a novel with more misgiving."

If this was true of the writer, whose name was, I now discovered, William Somerset Maugham, then it was equally true of me. Why Maugham began in doubt, I can't now remember, not having read the book in almost twenty years. But *I* was perplexed that night because I didn't even know what the book *was* for the first few pages—a novel, a memoir, a collection of essays—and didn't like what I read, because I was expecting of course something funny. But eventually I realized that this was a serious literary novel on which the recent film of Murray's had been based and that the novel, serendipitously, told the story of a young man trying to break with an unenlightened past and create a new identity.

The young man's name is Larry Darrell. His ambulance driving during World War I has traumatized him. When he returns to his native Chicago, he is not interested in reinhabiting the life he left behind, which holds for him an engagement to a beautiful, wealthy socialite and a high-paying job as a stockbroker. Needing to understand his pain, he rejects the role of well-to-do husband and goes in search of wisdom.

As Larry spent hours a day reading philosophy in the city library; as he lived in bohemian Paris; as he bummed around

Europe; as he traveled to an ashram in India; and as he experienced Enlightenment—as Larry did these things, I did them, over the next several nights, with him. I projected myself into his character: lived out my own struggles in his, explored a new identity as he fashioned one for himself, expanded into the knowledge of the West and the East, contemplated the Meaning of It All.

I wore the mask of this character. I donned the fakeness of his form. This playacting catalyzed energies, interests, passions I didn't know I had and perhaps didn't have, until I read the book.

I read about Larry studying Descartes, the great French philosopher. Doing so, I remembered that I once had read, maybe in a compendium of famous quotes, a line from Nietzsche, one of the only philosophers I had heard of at that time in my young life. (No doubt in a Christian context unfavorable to this devil who had pronounced God dead.) The quote went something like this: If grammar exists, so does God. Lying there reading about Larry puzzling over the old Cogito ergo sum, I was struck by the weirdness of Nietzsche's saying. I didn't know what it meant (I kind of do now), but I found its mystery riveting. What do verbs and prepositions (which my high school English teacher told me were anywhere a squirrel could jump) and interrogatives and subjunctives have to do with the whirlwind that chastened Job and Ezekiel's vision of the four-faced chariot?

Wondering over this inscrutable connection between skittering squirrels and heaven's fiery winds, I recalled that I had often thrilled to outlandish mind games. For instance, I had started, but not completed, an English paper on Hamlet and Benny Hill, the master of British dirty-old-man slapstick.

My uncooked intuition was, I guess, that manic metaphysical doubt and erotic craziness somehow go together.

As these memories rushed into my skull, there in that West Point barracks bed, I concluded, for the first time, that I was interested in *philosophy.*

Another night I read about Larry's stint on the Left Bank in Paris, and I remembered a book report I had to write, also in high school, on the French writer Albert Camus, who lived in the bohemian Rive Gauche during the years after World War II. While browsing through the Camus section in my school's small library, I saw one of his books, *The Myth of Sisyphus.* I opened it, skimmed a page, and saw, I *swear,* the sentence "A face that toils so close to stone is already stone itself." Recalling this passage from my darkened military bunk— ignorant of this sentence's meaning, too (I still don't really know what it signifies)—I conjured another scene from my past. I was camping with Baxter near a place called Dripping Rock. We got so bored that we threw unopened cans of Bluebird orange juice against the damp rock's face. Orange exploded onto the stone, flowed down lavalike into the mud. Six times we did this—three times each—and every time, I repeated this nursery-rhyme-mesmerizing nonsense in my head: "Fruit and the stone don't sing."

Larry Darrell in Paris, Camus's surreal stones, camping's accidental absurdity: as these things crashed together in my New Cadet head, I said to myself, "I love *poetry.*"

And more and more, while I was reading the *Razor,* old experiences I had forgotten arose and felt new, or experiences I had never even undergone presented themselves as if they had occurred. Whether real or not, the events constituted a novel past acting as preparation for the fresh future I was imagining, life as an intellectual, as a traveler, as a devotee of the mind. This future proved a magnetic force, pulling me inexorably toward it, humming in my inner ear: "This is who I have always been, but just didn't know it, my most essential yet secret self, hiding under the helmet."

Nightly renewed, this new identity—a mask as much maker as made—invigorated me during that month at West Point. It empowered me to carry out my duties though I hated them; to stand up to, and inwardly mock, the arguments of officers trying to talk me out of my decision to resign ("Do you know you're squandering your life, son?"); and to hold to my vision even though I was sequestered for three days in a room by myself (as were all who had chosen to leave), with nothing to do but think, never knowing when the plane ticket would come.

This, the transformation from jock to scholar, was a Pauline conversion, a jerking of my soul to the seventh heaven, so bright as to blind, that left me, on my own Damascus road, stunned, from my horse flung, lying on my back (like Caravaggio's Tarsusian), wondering if I would ever see or move again, before finding, seconds later, that my sight had returned more discerning, and my limbs more subtle and strong.

Let us say this is all true. It *is* true.

26.

Just been reading, for the tenth time or so, David Thomson's little essay on *The Big Sleep*, in which he praises Howard Hawks for his willingness to part with plot coherence in the name of making every scene interesting.

If you're dying to see what Bogey or Bacall will say or do next, who gives a rat's ass about who killed whom? Geiger, Brody, Mars. Agnes. Carmen. Harry Jones. Sean Regan. Porn. Gambling. A *bookstore* (?). They all run together and then vanish—save, on second thought, Elisha Cook's feisty Harry and Martha Vickers's nymphy Carmen—as we rivet our attention on B and B, with their erotically tense zingers and loopy, flirty humor.

By the film's end, when we behold their burning cigarettes side by side in the ashtray, as the two, after having survived great dangers, stare longingly at each other while the police sirens wail, we care nothing about anything except that these two beings exist and that is the most wonderful thing in the world.

It is moments like this—not meaning or moral or symbol or motif—that we will remember. And maybe, on third thought, General Sternwood's speech, in which the invalid—propped into aliveness by nostalgia and shame, as well as by the stifling heat of the greenhouse where Bogey's shamus Marlowe sweats and drinks brandy during the initial client interview—confesses, a bit dishonestly, that he seems "to exist largely on heat like a newborn spider." Any man who reminisces so fiercely—"I used to like [my brandy] with champagne. The champagne cold as Valley Forge and with about three ponies of brandy under it"—is hardly as fragile as an infantile arachnid. The martini I'm going to drink in five minutes, Bombay, very dry, up, olives, won't come close to the potion in this Sternwoodian reminiscence, conjured among the corrupt orchids that look too much "like flesh."

"Three ponies of brandy." Add that to Bacall's "I was beginning to think you worked in bed like Marcel Proust." And Bogey's "You're the second guy I've met today that seems to think a gat in the hand means the world by the tail."

Right now it appears that these are the things I'll remember (along with George Clooney's line in *O Brother, Where Art Thou?*: "I suppose it'd be the acme of foolishness to inquire if you had a hairnet" and John Huston's in *Chinatown*: "I believe they [the fish] should be served with the head").

Once, when I wanted to be a Scholar Who Knows Everything, I would have been sad over the loss of almost everything but style. Not, thanks to Thomson (and Greil Marcus and Geoff Dyer), anymore. Thomson's words and Hawks's directing help me justify my forgetting and the gin drinking that exacerbates the memory loss.

[Hawks] abandons story and genre as easily as one of [the girls in *The Big Sleep*] stepping out of her clothes, and says this is a movie about being a movie, about movieness. This is a kind of ongoing rehearsal or improvisation—very nicely done, mind you, there's no need for untidiness (however open in design, Hawks was a precisionist in shooting). [*The Big Sleep*] is a picture about its own process, the fun of making fun. That's why it [the film] needs to be all on sets: not as a way of drawing down the claustrophobia, the trap, of Fritz Lang's world, but as a sign that the whole thing is a game, an artifice, a celebration of acting, dialogue (as opposed to talk) and fantasizing. It is a dream about dreaming—maybe the best.

Is this a description of a kind of movie or a vision of how life should actually be lived? Wish Laurence Olivier, who was really far too British for Hawks's American vernacular, were here to answer. On the set of the 1976 film *Marathon Man*, Dustin Hoffman, who was playing a distance runner, was jogging furiously before a scene in which he was expected to depict physical exhaustion. Olivier, also starring, approached the young actor and, in his most elegant British accent, said, "My dear boy, have you ever considered acting?"

27.

In 1946, only weeks after Cary Grant, formerly known as Archie Leach, had finished filming the light romantic comedy *The Bachelor and the Bobby-Soxer*, he was approached by Alfred Hitchcock. Hitchcock had a film project to propose, a serious one that would once more pull Grant away from the comic fare that had largely made him famous (including Hawks's *Bringing Up Baby* and *His Girl Friday*). Hitchcock had already directed Grant in two psychologically complex films, *Suspicion*, from 1941, and *Notorious*, 1946. In both, Hitchcock did what no other director—not even the great Hawks or George Cukor—was able to do. He coaxed Grant's darker side from behind the tuxedoed sheen. In teasing out the actor's glooms, Hitchcock revealed the rift in the star's identity. One side of Grant was his former self, Leach, born into poverty in Bristol and bereft of his mother, Elsie, at age nine, when his father, Elias, wishing to marry another woman, had her secretly committed to an asylum for the insane. Elias told young Archie that his mum was on a long holiday, a lie that Archie didn't discover until thirty-one years later, when his name was Cary Grant.

Cary was, of course, the other side of the traumatized, depressed Archie. When the Bristol boy hit Hollywood in 1931, he created this persona, a smooth, elegant, upper-crust counter to his lowly past. Split and afflicted, Grant in Hitchcock's pictures before 1946 embodied the disquieting metaphysical conundrum troubling (and exhilarating) this book: when we say "I," no one knows who's really there. Hitchcock knew what he had uncovered, and this was why soon after Grant had completed another trifling comedy, he asked the entertainer to play Hamlet.

Grant turned the project down. He feared that he would be unable to perfect proper Shakespearean elocution. And he believed that he was, at the age of forty-two, too old to play the somber Dane, especially at a time when Hollywood was being overrun by youthful method actors like Montgomery Clift and Marlon Brando.

We might lament Grant's rejection as one of the great lost opportunities in cinema history. Surely, Grant would have made a thoroughly intriguing Hamlet, a scintillating mix of clever banter and cloyed intention. However, we need not feel this loss for long, for Grant did, in essence, end up performing Hamlet.

Some twelve years after Grant had passed on Hitchcock's request to play the traditional Hamlet, he went for the director's more hidden Hamlet, a character who appears to be a simple modern-day urban adman but who is actually terribly troubled by the question of identity. Indeed, he is sometimes, as when the vane points "north by northwest," insane, and reasonable only when the wind is "southerly." Then he knows "a hawk from a handsaw." This character exists in *North by Northwest* (1959), and his name is Roger Thornhill, or perhaps George Kaplan.

The antic disposition Hamlet adopts is but one of the many roles the Prince enacts in a play whose first line is "Who's there?" Hamlet tries on and casts off identities like Grant does his gorgeously tailored suits. The Dane is by turns a scholar, a courtly lover, an acting coach, a playwright, a soldier, a private investigator, a jester, a punster, a philosopher of infinitude and nutshells, a vengeful son, a forger, and, for only seconds, between Claudius's death and his own, a king. In crafting these and many other roles—such as melancholic, elegist, murderer—Hamlet embodies the exuberance and anxiety of forsaking the stable "who" for the dynamic "how": how to live, not what to be; how to remain Hamlet (for this isn't dissociative identity disorder) while experimenting with different modes of life.

Like Shakespeare his maker, who stayed William though he lived in characters as diverse as Iago and Rosalind, Hamlet intimates that we are at our best when we practice "negative capability," the ability to remain in "uncertainties, mysteries, doubts, without any irritable reaching after fact and reason." This is John Keats's concept, and he used it to describe the multifaceted Shakespeare. Keats could have applied the idea to Hamlet, too, of course, who came up with his own version: "the readiness is all." Be light on the feet, open and prepared to react to whatever arises, like a brilliant improvisational actor.

Keats is most Keats when he becomes the subjects of his odes—urns, nightingales, autumn—just as Shakespeare is most Bard in ranging from beggar to monarch, and Hamlet most Hamlet in spanning the virtual gamut of existence. In each case the multiplicity is informed by a certain style, angle, slant; habits of speaking and seeing; attitudes, quirks, tics, idiosyncrasies—the kinds of subtle characteristics that help us distinguish a Shakespeare poem from one by Christopher Marlowe, or Keats's verse from Coleridge's, or a Hamlet from an Othello.

The point is, you are most you, at your best, when you create the roles that make you feel most alive: witty, lyrical, speculative, loving, but also, and here's the rub, cynical, sarcastic, angry, muddled, sad—for negative states can be just as vital as positive ones. *Fullness* is the goal, myriad-mindedness (a happy phrase Coleridge conjured to describe Shakespeare): to be as varied and capacious as the cosmos. With this bigness, containing the most sublime and the low at once, you can hope that generosity will win out over the meanness, that you will foster the democratic, merciful embrace of what *is* as well as what *ought to be.* The best actor, Hamlet asserts, uses all gently.

Like the Dane, Grant was myriad and large in his panache, and he also knew that identity is not some unwavering "I-ness," but lies in creating the role that makes you most compelling, interesting. "To play yourself, your true self, is the hardest thing in the world." So Grant observed in an interview late in his life, and thus offered a strong retort to those who would criticize him for acting, regardless of role, like Cary Grant— even if this character is mica-flash quick with his protean wit. In fashioning his characters, Grant was faking his way to Hamlet-like authenticity: playing the parts that made him feel most whole.

Grant is more guru than movie star (Hamlet is more sage than character), modeling for us the fine art of creating a playful identity and never forgetting that it is an identity we play. Into what art are you turning your life? The mask

"Cary Grant," sadly, is taken. The "Hamlet" one, too. Don't worry: cut and paste, amalgamate, add, bend, fold, tear at the edges or paste in shellac, or start fresh, create the persona that will hopefully elicit what is most nuanced and charitable and full of grace.

28.

If he had lived in our time, Michel de Montaigne, the great sixteenth-century essayist (the originator of the essay genre, in fact), would have been an admirer of Grant. Montaigne spent most of his adult life learning how best to live through charming, playful, sly, skeptical, contradictory, improvisational, forgiving verbal experiments. As his mood took him, he might one day write about cannibals, another about the way to die well, still another on smells, and so on: warhorses, sleep, praying, drunkenness, cruelty, thumbs, monstrous children, cripples, vanity.

He loved thought games that startled him out of intellectual complacency; they sometimes got Dada: "When I play with my cat, who knows if I am not a pastime to her more than she is to me?"

Montaigne was comfortable with such silliness. "If others examined themselves attentively, as I do, they would find themselves, as I do, full of inanity and nonsense. Get rid of it I cannot, without getting rid of myself. We are all steeped in it, one as much as another; but those who are aware of it are a little better off—though I don't know."

29.

William James "Bill" Murray is a philosopher worthy of his namesake. A major moment in the development of his thought occurred in 1982, just after his then wife, Margaret "Mickey" Kelly, had given birth to their first child, Homer. A friend of Mickey's, the film director John Byrum, visited her in the hospital while she was recovering from the delivery. He gave her a book, perhaps to lighten, or enlighten, her convalescence. It was Maugham's *The Razor's Edge*. Byrum was thinking of making a film based on the book and so of risking a remake of the 1946 cinematic version, starring a war-weary Tyrone Power and the exquisite Gene Tierney, who was still fresh from *Laura* (in which she became a painting) and before her mental breakdowns of the fifties.

The next day Byrum was awakened by a phone call at 4:00 a.m. A man on the line said, "This is Larry, Larry Darrell." Like so many other actors who began as comics, such as John Belushi and Steve Martin, Murray wanted to play more dramatic roles. In this novel he had no doubt found on his tired wife's hospital bedstand was the perfect part. Byrum perhaps suspected Murray would be interested in portraying Darrell. (Why else would he have given the book to Mickey?) The director immediately cast Murray, and the two set off on a road trip across the United States, hoping to develop a script. They succeeded. The movie was soon financed by Columbia, reluctantly, since the company doubted the story's box-office potential. Murray had to promise to star in the studio's *Ghostbusters* to seal the deal.

Columbia was right to be skeptical: on a twelve-million-dollar budget, the film netted only six; it also received mostly negative reviews. One reason the film bombed, possibly the only reason: Larry Darrell's quest for enlightenment was rather undramatic because Bill Murray was *already enlightened.*

The light is there already, in his first recurring *SNL* character, Nick the Lounge Singer, performed consistently from 1977 to 1981. The man is a parody of the small-time seventies lounge singer: silk-shirted; gold-medallioned; mesotalented; hyperschmaltzy yet knowing it and weary of the role; torqueing easy listening standards into perky-weird medleys, mash-ups, and improvs; a low-grade Bobby Vinton; annoying and sweet at once, with charming earnestness and too-resilient-won't-shut-the-fuck-up–ness; chatting up the audience with painfully phony "and who do we have here?" talk; frequenter of low-traffic nightclubs, airport bars, Catskills ski lodges, and, in Nick's case, train car bars and, when really down on luck, prisons, knowing that retirement homes might be in his increasingly miserable future. What Murray brought to Nick the Lounge Singer was a compelling blend of desperate commitment (he *is* a *loser*) and a melancholy detachment that conveys "I know this is ridiculous and sad, but who really cares in this world in which nothing is not ridiculous and sad? Look, you can see it in my raised eyebrows, my eyes slightly askance, twinkling with my recognition of what you're thinking—*this is pitiful*—and acknowledging it, and even celebrating it, the cheesy sordidness, because it is kind of funny, in a way, and we might as well laugh instead of cry since it doesn't matter what we do."

The late Timothy White put this idea nicely in his 1988 piece "The Rumpled Anarchy of Bill Murray": the "quintessential Bill Murray portrayal has the actor simultaneously immersed in his role and commenting drolly on it." This tension between text and marginal note distinguished Murray from the spontaneous, unpredictable Belushi and the Ackroyd who could disappear entirely into his characters. Murray would, White continues, "permit viewers to see the actual process of assuming a character's essence—and the nakedness of the effort was startling."

30.

Murray's early acting might seem like camp, but it isn't. According to Susan Sontag, camp comes in two forms, "deliberate" and "naive." Deliberate camp occurs when a performer performs "in quotation marks." He acts artificially, frivolously, middle-class pretentiously, shockingly excessively, *way* over the top, all the while wink-winking, nod-nodding. Examples of this sort of camp are John Waters, Andy Warhol, Bette Midler, Rupaul, Paul Reubens (as Pee-wee Herman), Bugs Bunny, the B-52's, Queen, Adam West, *The Rocky Horror Picture Show*, *The Evil Dead*, *Big Trouble in Little China* (Kurt Russell as John Wayne!), and *Little Shop of Horrors*, featuring Bill Murray as a masochist who is more than a match for Steve Martin's ("I find a pussycat and bash in its head") sadist.

Opposed to deliberate camp is naive camp, campiness arising unintentionally, when productions are legitimately trying to be serious but failing so extravagantly they become funny or at least interesting. Sontag finds naive campy works to be far more satisfying than deliberate ones. Collections such as "The Ten Worst Movies of All Time"—in which you might find Busby Berkeley musicals (beautifully parodied in Preston Sturges's *Sullivan's Travels*, when Joel McCrea's character denigrates his earlier, shallow films *Hey Hey in the Hayloft* and *Ants in Your Pants of 1939*), Ed Wood's *Plan 9 from Outer Space*, *Monster a-Go Go* (which I must see), or *Showgirls* ("It must be weird, not having anybody cum on you")—often exemplify naive camp. (Though now that I think on it, *nothing* Paul Verhoeven makes is naive; I mean *RoboCop*, *Basic Instinct*, *Starship Troopers*. Scratch him from my half-thought-out list. And now I just watched the violin sequence in the Berkeley-choreographed *Gold Diggers of 1933*, which is charming, weird, and beautiful, perhaps not camp at all. Let's stick with *Plan 9* and *Monster a-Go Go*, I guess, even though, as I say, I haven't seen the latter.)

Deliberate camp blends fatigue and frivolity. Think of Warhol. For him, and for his pop art colleagues, Western art had pretty much worn itself out. After twenty-five hundred years of serious expression of truth, beauty, and goodness, there was nothing else to say; it had all been done. And even if an artist could achieve sublimity once more, the masses would be too shallow to notice or care, so inundated were they— we—with capitalistic longing for pleasing commodities, such as canned soups and packaged celebrities. Warhol believed that the only way to shock the audience out of its materialistic complacency was to re-present its favorite products as artworks in which the familiar images are slightly awry in texture and color. These campy exhibitions—silly things depicted with an awareness of their silliness—might startle us into seeing how shallow, how tired we've become.

Camp, then, no matter how entertaining and vaguely illuminating, is somewhat degraded, suggesting that there's nothing new under the sun, and so all we can do is just fiddle around

with what we've got, try to make it interesting enough to di-
vert ourselves for one more day, keep the boredom away, that
feeling that time is just one goddamn thing after another, like
channel surfing when you've seen each show already more
times than you can count, and the only way to hold back numb-
ing ennui is to mock the dialogue. If camp requires, as Sontag
claims, that we perceive "life as theater," with everyone simply
playing a prefabricated role, then the campy play is farcical:
nothing matters because it's all silly anyway.

31.

But what if not mattering doesn't mean *not* mattering, as in "Nothing's *important* enough to care about," but not *mattering*: nothing *is*, so there is not a thing to care about one way or the other? This half-ass koan's solution reveals why Bill Murray's performing is the opposite of camp: vital, sublime, transcendent, redemptive, wise.

Murray's Nick the Lounge Singer points to these qualities, but his Tripper Harrison, from his first film, the 1979 *Meatballs*, embodies them fully. Tripper is head counselor at Camp North Star, a bottom-shelf summer camp that annually closes its season by competing against the elite Camp Mohawk in the Olympiad, which includes traditional sporting events such as boxing, basketball, and cross-country, as well as more casual ones, like hot dog–eating and cup-stacking. As usual, Mohawk is crushing North Star at the end of day one of the two-day contest, 170 to 63.

That night, in the North Star lodge, Morty, the camp director, tries to motivate the kids with a flaccid cliché: "Just 'cause we're losing doesn't mean it's all over." After a counselor, Phil, retorts that such optimism is a load of crap, Tripper leaps up in front of the group. He is sporting white bell-bottom sweat-pants, held up by a bow-tied drawstring; a burgundy bowling shirt, trimmed in white and with the name "Dennis" stitched near the left lapel; and a *fez*, which he pulls off his head by the tassel and tosses into the crowd. He steps toward the fireplace, front and center, before all the campers and says, with a mixture of facetiousness (he knows it's a cliché) and earnestness (clichés, like it or not, have power), "That's just the attitude we don't need, Phil." Then, moving freely around the makeshift semicircular stage, he drops this admonishing tone and rises to football-coach motivational, his best Lombardi, shouting, with that compelling leader-of-men mix of reasoning, cajoling, and berating, "Sure, Mohawk has beaten us twelve years in a row. Sure, they're terrific athletes. They've got the best equipment that money can buy."

This is the setup, we think, to be followed by "But we can beat them because we have heart, character, spunk, gumption," etc. Tripper can't stick with the fire-up speech for long, though. Midway through the next sentence, which might have been the last part of the setup, his mind veers: "Hell, every team they're sending over here has their own personal masseuse"—pause—"not masseur, *masseuse*." Into this speech gap he falls, sliding from stern coach to cool dude, guy who sports Hawaiian shirts and hangs loose with the kids. He pictures, it seems, a hot chick massaging him, closes his eyes, nods approvingly, as a connoisseur of good pot might, after a long draw on a Jamaican hog leg. At the same moment that he shuts his eyes to savor his erotic reverie, he lifts his right hand to his heart and taps his chest gently, twice, with his index and middle fingers. Is he intimating that his heart, aroused like his loins, is palpitating?

Perhaps, but probably not. The lightness of the touch suggests otherwise, another shift, inward, to the heart of the matter, a shift signaled by what he says next: "But it doesn't matter." Now the coach, the dude fall away, and in their place is a crazed performance artist, mustering from somewhere deep the desperation of being alive in a world in which you are doomed to lose and be sad or to win and be sad. Though his words connect to the earlier Lombardi setup, his voice becomes increasingly hysterical, the unflappable leader, honest and righteous, morphing into a profoundly flappable bloke, willing to lie, cheat, con, in hopes—doomed—of beating the terrible odds. If the claim that summer camp kids can command personal masseuses is dubious, then the ensuing assertions, trickster-worthy (think Native American Coyote, Loki of the Norse, Chaplin's tramp, Puck), are beyond truth and falsehood. They are tall tales, redolent of old summer campfires, no, wait, more like surreal visions, each more hyperbolically weird than the last, concentrically circling, wider and wider, a cyclone forming, careening, rushing.

"Do you know," Tripper the Trickster yells, barely holding the intensifying shrillness in his chest, "that every Mohawk competitor has an electrocardiogram, blood and urine tests every forty-eight hours to see if there's any change in his physical condition? Do you know that they use the most sophisticated training methods from the Soviet Union, East and West Germany, and the newest Olympic power, Trinidad–Tobago? But [and here the abandonment of any pretense of control or logic, and the giving over to powers entrancing, shamanic, expressive only in the screaming chant where words once more become sounds and only sounds, barely holding to their semantics] it doesn't matter. It just doesn't matter [screaming

now, louder with each syllable]. IT JUST DOESN'T MAT-
TER. I tell you [now gesticulating like an epileptic, lunging
forward into the crowd, shaking a boy wearing a yellow hat,
knocking off the hat, grabbing the legs of the person to the
left, moving them side to side, screaming louder and louder]
IT JUST DOESN'T MATTER! IT JUST DOESN'T MAT-
TER! IT JUST DOESN'T MATTER [and now the group
joins in, in unison, louder and louder, clapping along with the
words, more and more passionately]. IT JUST DOESN'T
MATTER! IT JUST DOESN'T MATTER."

Just when the chanting reaches a violent pitch—will the
North Stars burst from the door, canoe like Vikings across
the lake, pillage the Mohawks?—Tripper reappears—how did
he get there?—at the center of the demicircumference and
morphs into an old-time revivalist preacher, out in a tent somewhere in Mississippi, his white suit soiled to gray, half-moons
of sweat swelling from his pits, selling salvation and snake oil.
He extends his arms to his sides, striking the crucifixion pose,
and wails, quieting the crowd, drawing out his syllables, just as
Robin Williams impersonating Ernest Angley later did: "And
eeeveeeen, and eeveen if we win, if we win [then a quick break
into the crazed piety, one shattering syllable "HA!" that might
start a long laugh but here reveals, in an instant so rapid you
almost miss it, that the Trickster is still in charge, can't help
blurting a guffaw over his own over-the-top performance;
back then to the evangelist, repeating himself, as all good evan-
gelists do, and repeating with apocalyptic exaggeration, anything to get the bodies down to the altar]. Eeveen if we win!
Eeveen if we play so far over our heads that our noses bleed for
a week to ten days. Eeveen if God in heaven above [and now he
points to heaven, Moses-like, just on the verge of going too

far, overacting, hamming it up to the point that everyone
knows it's a sham; but he stops short] comes down and points
his hand [he points to earth, still playing Moses, holding the
role, barely, together] at our side of the field. Eeveen if every
man, woman, and child held hands together and prayed for us
to win [hands by his sides now, waist-high, fists clenched, making us imagine the joining of hands], it just wouldn't matter
[why? Will he finally tell us why winning or losing won't matter? Yes] because all the really good-looking girls would still
go out with the guys from Mohawk 'cause they've got all the
money! [Are we deflated by this cynical assertion? No, because
the evangelist has become James Brown at the close of a roof-
raising, pelvis-exhausting, ankle-torqueing concert, falling
down in exhaustion, reminding us that the words in this case
don't mean shit, only the groove, the energy of the sound, the
meaning of meaninglessness, the thundering, "DA," of the
thunder, not its allegories of wrath and rain, listen to it, *listen*:
such are our thoughts as we watch Tripper turn his back to the
frenzied kids, who are now not chanting but dying to begin
again, and fling himself toward the hearth, bellowing like a
man who's just been shot or had an orgasm, and pick up a fire
log—so obviously fake, looks like Styrofoam—and bang it
rhythmically on the floor, a percussive accompaniment to the
lines, now as meaninglessly meaningful as the banging of wood
on wood, he yells, yells . . .] It just doesn't matter if we win or
we lose. IT JUST DOESN'T MATTER! [He bangs the log
harder and faster, hollers louder and faster, and the kids join in
again, clapping to the log beat, chanting once more.] IT JUST
DOESN'T MATTER! IT JUST DOESN'T MATTER! IT
JUST DOESN'T MATTER! IT JUST DOESN'T MATTER!
[Up Tripper jumps, makes his way into the bacchanal he has

created, pulls several campers by the hand into the sacred
semicircle; others follow, until the group has moved en masse
to Morty, the director, standing ecstatic to the right of the
fireplace, and lifted him up on their shoulders, as players a
victorious coach, or as believers the Jesus recently baptized by
Tripper, who moves in the waters of his sounds, eating honey
and wild locusts.]

32.

Why, we ask, does nothing matter? Maybe nothing—nothing as a concept, like "something" or "justice"—*matters*, is important. From where do all happenings come? From the fading into nothingness, as thirst disappears with drinking, of what came before. To where are all events flowing? To a future that does not yet exist; you can't quaff tomorrow's cocktails. What are events doing right now? There really aren't any, if an event is a duration of sameness, a "this" persisting in the blindingly quick flux of "thats." Each occurrence—the stirring of ice in gin, the sipping of its already fading chill—is really a blur of zeptoseconds, each different from those preceding it and those that will follow. It's not, as Heraclitus says, that you can't step into the same river twice. It is, as a good Buddhist would say, that you can't step into the same river even *once*.

Impermanence is, as Bhikkhu Bhodi, a distinguished Buddhist teacher, says, "the bedrock [odd word, given the slippery doctrine] for the Buddha's teaching, having been the initial insight that impelled the Bodhisattva to leave the palace in search of a path to enlightenment." For the Buddhist, impermanence "comprises the totality of conditioned existence, ranging in scale from the cosmic to the microscopic," from the "universe of immense dimensions evolving and disintegrating in repetitive cycles throughout beginningless time" to "our inescapable mortality, our condition of being bound to ageing, sickness, and death," to "the fact that all the constituents of our being, bodily and mental, are in constant process, arising and passing away in rapid succession from moment to moment without any persistent underlying substance."

In this universe of such radical ephemerality, what we take to be "things" are really "thinks." What is an olive? It is a gathering at one instant and at one point of multitudes of transient elements (themselves aggregates of scads of similarly lubricious energies): air, water, light, soil, chlorophyll, weather, geology, geography. To conceive of this node of being, a tiny knot on an infinite net, as a self-same, durable object is obviously to dwell in error, just as claiming that a knot can exist without a rope is a mistake, or that an eddy is extant absent an ocean. And the error of saying—"This is an olive"—is compounded because any given perception is as vastly disparate as the perceiver, dependent upon height; weight; strength, or lack thereof, of vision; angle of vision; mood; temperament; time of day, week, year, decade; position, be it local or global; where the butterfly's wings flap. Percipient, perceiver: there's no such thing as either, again, if a thing is an object or event that endures in a self-same form.

So as Borges's Funes knew, what we call events and objects are illusions, images and concepts we construct in order to feel more secure, more comfortable in this inexorably fluxional cosmos. But these illusions are inadequate to the task, stop signs blown down the minute they are put up, anchors that immediately lose their density, float away, dams burstable, nets trying to catch the air. Not only are they, our concepts and images, doomed to fail, but they are also destined to sadden. Our cognitions are markers, and this alone, of thwarted desire. We ground our ideas of happiness on the stability of objects and events: beautiful houses or cars or clothes, the making of money or the gaining of public success, a sense of an enduring "self" that grows, like a tree. This notion of happiness is patently unreasonable in an insecure universe, but we can't accept this state of affairs. We blind ourselves to what is true—there are no things—and place our hope in things, which are really, remember, *thinks*. These thinks, though, turn out to be just as transient as the forces they attempt to slow, corral, control. So the tools we fashion to comfort us actually cause suffering, encouraging urges that will remain forever unfulfilled.

The question now is, What is this *nothing* that matters, in a world in which nothing *matters* (where nothing is solid, graspable, durably material)? The answer lies in the famous Heart Sutra, the essential text of Mahayana Buddhism, which Allen Ginsberg chanted on the first day of that Beat lit class I took with him during the fall of 1991. The center of the sutra goes like this:

Form is emptiness and the very emptiness is form; emptiness does not differ from form, form does not differ from emptiness; whatever is form, that is emptiness, whatever is emptiness, that is form, the same is true of feelings, perceptions, impulses and consciousness . . . [I]n emptiness there is no form, nor feeling, nor perception, nor impulse, nor consciousness; no eye, ear, nose, tongue, body, mind; no

forms, sounds, smells, tastes, touchables or objects of mind;
no sight-organ element, and so forth, until we come to: no
mind-consciousness element; there is no ignorance, no extinction of ignorance, and so forth, until we come to: there
is no decay and death, no extinction of decay and death.
There is no suffering, no origination, no stopping, no path.
There is no cognition, no attainment and non-attainment.

"Emptiness" here is a translation of the word *sunyata*, which
means "nothingness" or "zeroness." It is the term for the void
at the heart of matter, the no-thing-ness from which moments
arise and into which they vanish, the insubstantiality of these
actual moments. The word also signals the absence at the core
of these very words I'm using to describe it, words nothing but
sonic vibrations, themselves undulations of bodiless forces
crisscrossing the cosmos itself, the cosmos but a vast pattern of
an energy including millions of other universes, each itself a
gigantic vortex of even vaster powers, potencies upon potencies, deeps upon abysses.

The image many Buddhists favor to picture this infinite
interdependence of coreless, ephemeral forms is the Jewel Net
of Indra, composed entirely of crystalline gems. Each gem re-
flects and is reflected by all other gems in the network, sym-
bolizing the idea that all forms in the universe depend upon
and are dependent upon all others for their appearance and
thus that no one form is independent, self-sustaining, essential, but rather a node made of images that are themselves
nodes made by images, and so on. The universe is a hall of mirrors, a cabinet of illusions, a *Lady from Shanghai* final scene played
in an endless and immense loop, with this exception: nothing,
Orson, lies behind the glass.

But the emptiness is not simply the annihilation of form; it is also the origin of form—plenitude as much as void. It is the hole creating the cup; the ghostly triangles necessary for the wagon wheel; the sculptor's divots and the writer's blank page. It, this creative nothingness, is the nightly blackout from which the dream's psychedelics leap and the space at the monstrous cyclone's spine and the "no" essential for "yes" and those zeros, ovals of not-something-ness, needed to expand one to one million octillions.

When you realize the mattering of nothing, and the nothingness of matter (the emptiness originating the forms, the forms fading into the void), what are you to do?

Try for the wisdom of insecurity; this, Alan Watts believes, is enlightenment. Remain calm amid the flux because you know and accept there's nothing but flux. Don't get riled when you lose everything, because you know all is already lost. Stay unaroused, too, when the ship comes in, since you've already got everything you need, which is nothing. Against Watts's wisdom is the craving for security, sweating to hang on to what you've got as it is inevitably slipping away, or laboring to get something when you already possess everything you need. You try to be spontaneous; you can't be, since you're straining to let go of straining. The thing is, you're already part of the flow—you breathe without making yourself breathe; you grow hair, pump blood. You just won't let your mind relax into what your body is doing.

Obviously, to relax without becoming a slug, to act without growing tense, are difficult states to achieve, elite-athlete hard: grace under pressure, getting into the zone, giving 110 percent while not even breaking a sweat. This disciplined loafing requires viewing life as a dramatic performance, in which we enter fully into a given role, feeling sorrow and joy, affection and disdain, all the while knowing that nothing, really, is happening, that we'll step into the greenroom when the play ends, unscathed, balanced, ready to kick back with George Dickel.

Murray's Nick the Lounge Singer finds this path between motion and stillness. He shifts from treacly balladeer to seedy crooner to emcee hopped up on faux bonhomie to Phil Donahue–esque talk show host to sad sack never-has-been, copping the bottom-shelf doppelgängerdom of a Neil Diamond–Tom Jones–Michael Bolton mash-up, all the while subtly telegraphing, through glance or overemphasis of gesture or phrase, that he, Murray, or Nick, or amalgamation of two, knows what's going on, realizes that this is a performance with no other purpose than to be a performance. Murray as Tripper is even more deliberate in this practice, not only juggling multifarious masks like a circus master but also delivering in words the message he fleshes: it just doesn't matter.

So when Murray came to play Larry Darrell, a young man laboring to walk the edge of the razor, the drama was done, since Murray had been balanced on this line for years already. To those expecting drama—struggle and resolution—the film was boring. To those connoisseurs of Murray's acting just to act, with no end in the offing, the movie formed a minor masterpiece. Such appreciators, including, gentle reader, this neurotic author, have come to relish Murray's roles in other films that actually emphasize the pleasure—as Wallace Stevens does in a poem—of merely circulating, playing with no concern for the outcome. There is Jim Jarmusch's *Broken Flowers*, in which we get to watch Murray simply *be*—take naps, ride planes, look at cars, buy bottled water—as he comes to realize that the present moment is all that exists, which of course means that nothing exists, since the present, the instant you say "present," is already gone. And there is Harold Ramis's *Groundhog Day*, where Murray relives the same day over and over again, until he creates a persona that can love and be loved, each day already knowing what's going to happen and so performing his life as an actor would a script, improving his acting a bit each day, until he becomes a compelling and compassionate being.

33.

In April 1870, when he was twenty-eight, William James, already deep in a debilitating depression, a symptom of what he later termed the sickness of soul, underwent an hallucination as harrowing as any horror story.

I went one evening into a dressing-room in the twilight to procure some article that was there; when suddenly there fell upon me without any warning, just as if it came out of the darkness, a horrible fear of my own existence. Simultaneously there arose in my mind the image of an epileptic patient whom I had seen in the asylum, a black-haired youth with greenish skin, entirely idiotic, who used to sit all day on one of the benches, or rather shelves against the wall, with his knees drawn up against his chin, and the coarse gray undershirt, which was his only garment, drawn over them inclosing his entire figure. He sat there like a sort of sculptured Egyptian cat or Peruvian mummy, moving nothing but his black eyes and looking absolutely non-human. This image and my fear entered into a species of combination with each other[.] THAT SHAPE AM I, I felt, potentially. Nothing that I possess can defend me against that fate, if the hour for it should strike for me as it struck for him. There was such a horror of him, and such a perception of my own merely momentary discrepancy from him, that it was as if something hitherto solid within my breast gave way entirely, and I became a mass of quivering fear.

The moment broke James's life in two. After the incident, he continues,

the universe was changed for me altogether. I awoke morning after morning with a horrible dread at the pit of my stomach, and with a sense of the insecurity of life that I never knew before, and that I have never felt since. It was like a revelation; and although the immediate feelings passed away, the experience has made me sympathetic with the morbid feelings of others ever since. It gradually faded, but for months I was unable to go out into the dark alone.

Those of us afflicted with chronic depression (the doctors call it clinical, as if it were taking place or could be cured in a sanitary white large room) have suffered such moments of our own, but rarely have our horrors (I have had one) borne the burden of being the same ghoulish vision, almost to the detail, that our own fathers endured.

When William had been in the world for two and a half years—and his brother Henry thirteen months—the father, also named Henry, had a horrific collapse of his own. This was in May 1844, when the family was living in a cottage near

Windsor, England, called Frogmore. Thirty years later, Henry Sr. recalled the terror:

> [H]aving eaten a comfortable dinner, I remained sitting at the table after the family had dispersed, idly gazing at the embers in the grate, thinking of nothing, and feeling only the exhilaration incident to a good digestion, when suddenly—in the lightning flash as it were—"Fear came upon me, and trembling, which made all my bones to shake." To all appearance it was a perfectly insane and abject terror, without ostensible cause, and only to be accounted for, to my perplexed imagination, by some damned shape squatting invisible to me within the precincts of the room, and raying out from his fetid personality influences fatal to life.

This "damned shape," eerily akin to the monstrous "SHAPE" his son witnessed twenty-six years later, wrecked the next two years of Henry's life, a period the older James termed his "vastation," an archaic version of "devastation," a Job-like affliction. (Note his quoting of Job 4:14 to describe his fear, a passage Søren Kierkegaard later invoked for his equally terrifying *Fear and Trembling*, in which he wonders what kind of God would command Abraham to kill his boy Isaac.) Henry saw his emergence from this depression as a second birth.

William referenced his father's collapse in a footnote to his printed description of his own mental disintegration, appearing in his 1902 *Varieties of Religious Experience*, where he actually attributes his dreadful experience to another sufferer. Like his father, William saw his healing as resurrection but likely had to labor more arduously to achieve his rebirth because he lacked his Swedenborgian progenitor's belief in a merciful God. In fact, a primary source of his despair was his fear that the universe was void of ultimate goodness, meaning, and purpose and that he didn't have the will to face such a world honestly and thrive.

James overcame his hopelessness through a heroic implementation of Hans Vaihinger's philosophy of "as if," later embodied, though James didn't know it (how could he?), by Murray's creation of a new persona for every critical pulsation. Soon after his nightmare, James writes: "I think that yesterday was a crisis in my life. I finished the first part of Renouvier's second Essais and see no reason why his definition of Free Will—'the sustaining of a thought *because I choose to* when I might have other thoughts'—need be the definition of an illusion . . . My first act of free will shall be to believe in free will . . ." What is real: beside the point. What one *believes* is real is decisive.

I am William James. I believe that the universe is ruinous and I can't do anything about it. I can't prove if this belief is valid or not, but it certainly creates undeniably palpable encounters—with mental anguish, weapons I might use to kill myself. Then again, I am William James. I will myself to believe that I am free to shape my life in ways less destructive, that I can perhaps create a flourishing existence, in which green-fleshed asylum wards recover their healthful flush, and revolvers—antique, burnished in the twilight—hang over the fireplaces of the philosopher's study, decorating the room, giving it depth, seriousness, heritage. I act as if this belief were true. I don the mask of the resurrected. The sick becomes well. Weapons turn artifacts.

After his reentry into life through faking to live— performing as though he were free—James fashioned original theories on emotions. He concluded that physical action precedes feeling, not the other way around. We don't laugh because we are joyful; we are joyful because we laugh. (This idea remains integral to psychology, serving as a core principle for cognitive behaviorism.) It follows: if I want to be happy, I should smile more; my content will rise up to meet my form, just as a life will reach for a belief, a character will conform to clothing.

These insights provided the foundation for the philosophy for which James is most famous, pragmatism, based on the idea that there's no such thing as TRUTH—universal and unchanging—but rather various interpretations of the world, some of which are temporarily true in that they are useful, not just physically but psychologically and spiritually. Truth *happens* to those interpretations of life that empower us and those around us to enjoy more capacious, charitable, beautiful, vigorous existences. These veracious happenings are necessarily temporary, since the world is radically evanescent, constantly requiring new ideas to make sense of new circumstances, to transform them into horizons toward which purposeful meaning can emerge. To use the words of the literary critic Ross Posnock (who locates William's ideas in the late novels of his brother Henry), self in this perspective is "contingent, inseparable from the process of experimental inquiry and interpretation," constantly interacting with the world, composed of "open and revisable events." The void inspires value. Successful improvisation is wisdom.

34.

Our man William James, whom I can't seem to let go of (the philosopher A. N. Whitehead, who knew him personally, called him an "adorable genius"), experienced firsthand the San Francisco earthquake of 1906. He was sixty-four. He awakened to the rumbling; his hotel was shaken, he wrote, like a rat by a terrier. He did not despair, however, or descend into death shivers. He exulted in the force. He roared, "Go it. Go it stronger."

James would have said to Julia Lohmann, "Go it."

Lohmann, a contemporary German artist, was commissioned to fashion a work for the street-level windows of the London headquarters of the Wellcome Trust, a foundation for health research. Fittingly, she settled on a female figure, traditionally an icon of bodily vitality and beauty.

How would she create the wholesome elegance? With paint or pencil, pixel or plastic? No, with *bacteria*. Lohmann made two immense reclining nudes from nine thousand petri dishes, each of which was teeming with living microbes. Diseases thriving on perfect circles of bright orange or red or pink, arranged into urban-transforming Venusian splendor: what more potent, enthusiastic, and generous-hearted conversion of destruction into exuberance, mindless decay into meaning, life into art, could there be?

35.

To convert rot to exuberance: this is the spirit of the placebo effect, occurring when positive mental energy heals what ails you. Is James an adherent of such spooky science? I don't quite know, but the possibility is intriguing, as is the case of one of the earliest and most notorious believers in the placebo, that of Franz Anton Mesmer, who spent the last decades of the eighteenth century placing the mentally and the physically ill in what he hoped were healing trances.

Soon after completing his medical studies at the University of Vienna, Mesmer in 1766 published a book claiming that an invisible force, animal magnetism, pervades all matter. When the magnetic powers in our bodies are aligned with the northern and southern poles of the universe, we are healthy. Discord with these cosmic coordinates results in disease, physical and mental. The cure requires a return to harmony.

Mesmer attempted to restore the concord through the process that now bears his name, mesmerism. He would sit facing the patient, touch his knees to hers, hold her thumbs in his hands, stare intensely into her eyes. He would move his hands around her body, about an inch from her flesh, much like a modern specialist in Reiki. This motion massaged her *poles*. He might also press his hands against her flesh, just below the diaphragm. Combined with his robe, a magic wand, and music from his glass harmonica, these procedures frequently hypnotized patients. While they were under, Mesmer would elicit conversations on their maladies, trying to put them through a "crisis" that would purge the bad energy and once more allow the good freely to flow. He might tell the patient that her fever was draining out of her body, and she might awaken believing that indeed it had and feel better immediately.

After failing to cure a blind girl in Vienna, Mesmer fled to Paris, where he continued his work. He became a sensation and soon had more patients than he could handle. To meet the overwhelming demand for his services, he constructed "baquets," tubs containing magnetized materials to which patients could connect via several protruding iron rods. Once he even magnetized a tree, from which patients formed a human chain, one link passing the power to the next. Of course Mesmer became rich and famous and probably enjoyed the convulsions of the scantily clad young females (thick clothes blocked the flow) he often treated.

So great was the furor over Mesmer that it piqued the interest of King Louis XVI. In 1784, he commissioned a group of scientists, including Benjamin Franklin and Antoine Lavoisier, to investigate. The group found no evidence for animal magnetism but did not discount the beneficial results of the hypnotism. It concluded that "imagination" somehow caused the results.

Franklin and Co. happened upon the placebo effect. A

recent *Radiolab* episode featured several stunning stories of the power of placebo, ranging from the case of Mesmer to a physician who cured a terrible skin disease through hypnosis to the ministrations of medicine men to the restorative powers of pill colors. Researchers have concluded that believing you are being cured can cause the brain to produce the chemicals that compose many of our drugs, including opiates. The problem is, placebo curing works only about 25 percent of the time, and success is difficult to predict.

Still, the placebo effect demonstrates the power of the mind to shape matter, fiction to create fact, theater (Dumbledorean robes and phony magic wands and Enyaesque music) to dictate the examining room (where crisp white coats, stethoscopes, and Muzak usually reign).

I think that's as far as I want to go into placebo, because if I were to keep pushing, I'd find myself staring at Phineas Parkhurst Quimby, the mesmerist from Maine who rose to fame in the middle of the nineteenth century, under whose tutelage Mary Baker Eddy developed the ideas and practices that resulted in Christian Science, which is based on the idea that all diseases are purely mental and so curable by positive thinking.

James, sick-souled, was actually taken aback by the hyperpositive attitude of Christian Scientists, who were becoming legion in the late nineteenth and early twentieth centuries. James called them "moonstruck with optimism." The psychologist was too much of a realist to put much stock in cosmic harmony. The universe is fractured, turbulent, painful, no matter how you look at it. Still, James shares one basic assumption with Mesmer, Quimby, and Eddy, as well as with Norman Vincent Peale, whose Power of Positive Thinking movement was significantly influenced by Eddy: "reality" is just as mental as it is physical.

James would probably even agree with Peale that repeating happy affirmations can make you successful in life. But from Peale it is a short step to all manner of New Age spirituality, with its astrology, parapsychology, chanting, herbs, Druids, Wicca, Aquarius, ambient music, crystals, incense, reincarnation, all of which is fine, really, and probably totally conducive to a good life, but which I find creepy and soft-headed and divorced from the nit and grit that give me traction in life. James would feel the same way, I think, knowing that it's the parts of life that appear the most unmagical that stimulate the most powerful narratives, those of rebirth and redemption.

And anyway, while I'm speaking of creepy, ever seen a mesmerized man? You don't have to watch *The Cabinet of Dr. Caligari* to realize that a hypnotized person is devoid of personal agency and so no different from a machine. And that's where the real terror begins: when we don't know the difference between a human and an android. Sleep in a room full of puppets or dolls one night, and you'll see what I mean, or stare at a mummy a long time in a dark museum just about ready to close, or get lost in a robot factory.

Or read a biography of Descartes, who believed that our bodies are mechanisms somehow inhabited by mind, the ghost in the machine. In 1649, Descartes shipped from Holland to Sweden. He was bound for the palace of Queen Christina in Stockholm, where he was to become philosophy tutor to the court. Once aboard the vessel, Descartes told passengers that his young daughter, Francine, was accompanying him. But as the ship pushed north, no one set eyes on the girl. Folks, especially the crew, began to talk. A horrible storm broke out. Amid the chaos, no one could find Descartes and his daughter. Fearing the worst, sailors burst into the philosopher's cabin. No one was there. But wait. A large box was standing in the corner. Curiosity overcame caution, and the men pried it open. Inside was a figurine of a small girl. One of the sailors picked it up. Its eyes opened. He dropped it and ran out of the room, the other crewmen following. They immediately reported this incident to the captain. A superstitious man, he concluded that this unnatural thing had caused the storm. He ordered the sailors to toss the girl into the ocean. How Descartes reacted to the loss of his automaton, no one knows. But he probably took it hard, because the doll was a substitute for a fully human daughter, also named Francine, who had died of scarlet fever ten years earlier, at the age of five.

36.

Annie Dillard's famous opening to *Pilgrim at Tinker Creek*, in which a tomcat freshly returned from his nocturnal prowling leaps through the writer's morning window, lands on her chest, and awakens her by kneading her bosom, is not based on fact. The cat, to continue, stamps bloody paw stains on Dillard's white gown. They remind her of rose petals. Dillard admitted at a writing conference that said tomcat never clawed her awake but did scratch to consciousness a student of hers, from whom she borrowed the tale, with permission. The nature writer seized on the story as parable-ready and used it to introduce her exuberantly harrowing book on nature's violence and beauty.

No one likely would dream of taking Dillard down, not at least for a little fibbing compensated by potent poetry. But what of James Frey, who fabricated details, especially surrounding drug addiction and arrest, in his memoir *A Million Little Pieces*? Oprah Winfrey, reality-committed, beat him floorward on live TV, pinning on him the charge of "liar." It stuck, and disciples of truth throughout the land rejoiced over her successful inquisition of the inauthentic, with Maureen Dowd of *The New York Times* encapsulating the mood among Those Who Read: "It was a huge relief, after our long national slide into untruth and no consequences, into Swift boating and swift bucks, to see the Empress of Empathy icily hold someone accountable for lying." Oprah's opprobrium seemed to *annihilate* the prevaricator's career—Larry King's verb, that—but Frey, like Annie's feline, has proved not yet killable, writing a novel, *Bright Shiny Morning*, that Sara Nelson, in *Publishers Weekly*, called "un-put-downable, a real page turner, in what may come to be known as the Frey tradition."

What is the line between Dillard as legit literary nonfictionalist and Frey as lowdown fabricator? Is Dillard's slight rearranging of "what happened" a forgivable little fib in the service of a deeper literary "truth"? Then is Frey's more whopper-size exaggeration a pernicious violation of the reader's trust, in the name of bestsellerdom?

These are important questions to ask in this time when literary hoaxes far more extreme than Frey's are common. In 2008 Margaret Seltzer, aka Margaret B. Jones, published a memoir about her struggles as a half–Native American, half-white gang member in South-Central L.A., even though she is a middle-aged Caucasian who grew up wealthy in the San Fernando Valley. From 2000 to 2004 Laura Albert, another middle-aged woman, published three "real-life" novels under the guise of JT LeRoy, a cross-dressing, HIV-positive teenage boy who was once a prostitute, and even convinced a friend to play the role of JT in public. And in 2008 Herman Rosenblat fabricated key elements in his memoir about falling in love with his wife in the Buchenwald concentration camp.

For those who've read their Derrida and Debord, their

Vaihinger and James, their Hayden White and Gazzaniga, the distinction society has deployed to condemn the Freys and Seltzers—between fiction, or illusion, and fact, which is reality—might seem crude. And for those who have studied Barthes's famous essay "The Death of the Author," even to believe that one man or woman is the responsible creator and owner of a given text is jejune.

But the most hard-core proponent of constructivism—the world is made, not found—would wince if someone stole his research and then the thief tried to pass it off as his own. And the constructivist would do more than wince if the work he did actually publish under his name generated profit, but he was barred from claiming the money. He couldn't be the author, after all, all authors being now dead.

Even in a world where fact is fiction and fiction fact, we require a standard by which to call some liars and others truth-tellers, to say that this is *mine*, that yours. One way to do this is to say that sure, on an epistemological level, we can never grasp reality as it is, but on a more practical level, we know that certain physical events occurred and others have not. We've agreed as a society that those physical events that actually happened—like jail time or gang wars—are real, while those that didn't take place are not. To claim in this society that something that occurred did not, or that something that didn't go down did, constitutes a lie, and society has generally agreed that lying is harmful—regardless of motive—because lying destroys other distinctions essential for a society's success: between legitimate criminal evidence and bogus; ownership and fraud; trust and the lack.

So, according to this pragmatic model, which James would likely endorse, we can distinguish between truth and lie and condemn the latter, even if the standards are not universally true but temporary and probably arbitrary. But the question remains: Why would we condemn Frey while we celebrate Dillard?

Both writers are engaged in a genre known as creative non-fiction, which encompasses literary memoirs, essays, nature writing, journalism, and travel writing. Works in this genre combine fact and fiction. While authors aspire to be faithful to what actually happened, inwardly or outwardly, they select, compress, expand, and arrange the data according to literary conventions like plot, point of view, character development, symbolism, tone, and style. Creative nonfiction reports accurately as well as aesthetically.

Honoring this genre, we don't hold Dillard and Frey to the same standards of accuracy to which we would hold a historian or a war correspondent. But even if we allow these writers imaginative room, we still expect them to stay close to actual occurrences. It is one thing for Frey to tweak his struggles with addiction to achieve maximum literary power; it is another for him to fabricate experiences entirely and make them central to his story. Because Dillard remains close to actual happenings for almost her whole book—scientific laws, places anyone can visit, parts of her history easily verifiable—we forgive her a little straying, especially when it results in such sublimity and conveys her themes so gorgeously.

We might further distinguish between Frey's extreme fictionalizing and Dillard's more minimal by speculating on their intentions. We could assert that Frey fabricated for financial reasons, knowing that a memoir on the harrowing experiences of an addict would probably sell better than a novel on the same, and we could conversely conclude that Dillard fudged a bit for worthier literary reasons. But such speculations would be dubious, first of all because it is almost impossible to ascertain the full depth of anyone's intentions—so entangled with unconscious and conscious motives are intentions—and second of all because it is quite possible that Frey's intentions were more literary than mercenary, and Dillard's the opposite.

Ultimately, the most compelling way to distinguish between Frey's fiction-making and Dillard's is to claim that one is more *aesthetically* successful than the other. Perhaps readers condemned Frey because he violated their aesthetic expectations. Frey chose the form of the confessional memoir, in particular the memoir of suffering and redemption, most notably exemplified by Augustine's *Confessions*, Harriet Jacobs's *Incidents in the Life of a Slave Girl*, Thomas Merton's *Seven Storey Mountain*, and Malcolm X's *Autobiography*. For such a memoir to succeed, it must express sincerity, authenticity, one person revealing his or her deepest agonies to others. Since Frey's language performed such states so convincingly, readers at first generally loved the book. But once they discovered that these linguistic moves lacked physical reality, they felt betrayed: what they most wanted in a memoir of this kind—raw honesty—had vanished.

Dillard decided on another form, the nature essay, whose most powerful practitioners include Henry David Thoreau, John Muir, Edward Abbey, and Peter Matthiessen. Here the contract with the reader differs. We look in such books not so much for sincerity as for acute observation of place, lyrical descriptions of relationships between human and globe, transformations of this rock or that river into a symbol of the whole. If the writer delivers, we don't care so much about accuracy. So what if Thoreau didn't really drive his nails with one blow, as bent nails around his Walden Pond home suggest? He lived on the water and it gave him life, and in his words he made the water live. That is enough.

Is the most useful standard of truth aesthetic? Is Dillard's fiction "truer" than Frey's because it is more beautiful—more exhilarating to readers, whose longings it generously fulfills, more intense, capacious, complex, more expressive of what lived experience is like, soothing and horrible, chaotic as well as ordered, so lovely you can barely stay inside your skin and so painful you'd just as soon pave forests as trudge in them? Is Frey's fashioning false because it is not as exquisite, disappointing readers in its voiding of the genre contract and so striking them as phony, selfish, flat, an account not of pain and transcendence but of manipulation, deception?

Has a truth just happened to an idea?

37.

Five years after I resigned from West Point, a truth happened to me: I learned that to be intellectual means being weird. In college (Appalachian State University in Boone, North Carolina), I was still too immured in my fine-young-man upbringing to try on outlandishness. I was quite staid, applying the inflexible discipline to my studies that I had once applied to football. I worked twelve hours a day, sometimes more, on Eliot, Wordsworth, Milton, Shakespeare, Donne, Chaucer; turned in papers early, after putting them through three drafts; never missed class, never was late; spoke at least twice during each class discussion; performed eager intellectual behavior, with brow furrowing and knowing nodding; brownnosed the profs; and got what I wanted at that time more than sex or booze, the A. "I might fail in the army and football," I said to myself, "but I sure as hell won't fail as a disciple of Larry Darrell."

It wasn't until I reached graduate school that I mustered the guts to get weird. I decided one day in 1991, during my first semester in the Ph.D. program in the Graduate Center of the City University of New York, that I would make my mind *labyrinthine*.

I was sitting in a seminar taught by Angus Fletcher, the most brilliant person I've ever met. I can't remember the course. Doesn't matter, because all the courses Angus taught were really about the mind of Angus, exhilaratingly labyrinthine: baroque, otherworldly, expansive, far out, cosmic, uncanny.

It was in Angus's classes that I first read Borges's collection *Labyrinths*, which includes "Funes the Memorious." The collection also features "Pierre Menard, Author of the Quixote," which is about a translator of Cervantes who immersed himself so deeply into his rendering that he wanted to reproduce, line by line, in the Spanish of Cervantes, the exact *Don Quixote* itself. "He did not," Borges's narrator writes, "want to compose another Quixote—which is easy—but *the Quixote itself*. Needless to say, he never contemplated a mechanical transcription of the original; he did not propose to copy it. His admirable intention was to produce a few pages which would coincide—word for word and line for line—with those of Miguel de Cervantes." According to the narrator, Menard accomplished this. Here is an example of his work, set beside Cervantes's own text. There is also commentary by the narrator.

It is a revelation to compare the *Don Quixote* of Pierre Menard with that of Miguel de Cervantès. Cervantes, for example, wrote the following (Part I, Chapter IX):

. . . truth, whose mother is history, rival of time, depository of deeds, witness of the past, exemplar and adviser to the present, and the future's counselor.

This catalog of attributes, written in the seventeenth century, and written by the "ingenious layman" Miguel de Cervantes, is mere rhetorical praise of history. Menard, on the other hand, writes:

> . . . truth, whose mother is history, rival of time, depository of deeds, witness of the past, exemplar and adviser to the present, and the future's counselor.

History, the *mother* of truth!—the idea is staggering. Menard, a contemporary of William James, defines history not as delving into reality but as the very font of reality. Historical truth, for Menard, is not "what happened"; it is what we *believe* happened. The final phrases—*exemplar and adviser to the present, and the future's counselor*—are brazenly pragmatic.

I need not say that Menard's version captures the primary argument of this book, *Keep It Fake*, rather beautifully, much more so, in fact, than Cervantes's own text and mine.

One day in class, Angus actually read this exact passage, in a resonant, slightly hesitant, melancholy yet affirmative voice, the same voice with which he one day read Andrew Marvell's longish "The Garden" (in which the mind annihilates "all that's made / To a green thought in a green shade"), after which the class sat in *stunned silence*, before Angus gave a gentle chuckle, to save us from awkwardness but also to acknowledge that something really wondrous had just occurred. Remarkably, in reading both Borges passages—one by Cervantes, the other by Menard—in *exactly* the same way, he captured perfectly their vast distance in depth and meaning.

Once he had finished—again with the class sitting in *stunned silence*, but not as stunned or silent since the passage wasn't as long as Marvell's poem—he said, after pausing a few seconds, "Isn't that uncanny?"

I knew what this word signifies in Sigmund Freud's famous essay "Das Unheimliche," or "The Uncanny": the return of the repressed, in such a way that what has returned—an unspeakable fear, perhaps, or a forbidden desire—is both unfamiliar, because it has been hidden below consciousness a long time, and familiar, since it has been an integral part of the consciousness it has shaped. Uncanny moments: walking into the bathroom in the middle of the night—you've *really* got to go—accidentally turning on the light, and seeing, in the mirror, someone who looks like you but is not you. Freud would say that you have experienced how your soul might appear once you die, as a near double of your living self, and you are terrified and fascinated.

I think Angus meant that Borges's passage is uncanny because it elicits both fear of and desire for the double: not wanting to die; longing to become a soul. The passage is also perhaps uncanny in another way: it dredges the horror of the possibility that it's *all* a recording, that we all are simply mimicking, word for word, gesture for gesture, scenes that have taken place in the past but making these scenes seem to mean different things. At the same time, the passage unearths desire for the very situation, since if we are simply acting out, without choice, prefabricated scripts, we are released from the burdens of responsibility.

(Repetition *is* horrifying. Think of Stanley Kubrick's *The Shining*, which features the labyrinth made of shrubbery. In the film, the ghosts of the two daughters the caretaker Grady hacked to pieces look exactly alike and are dressed the same in little-girl yellow party dresses, though one sibling is slightly taller than the other. The picture also features Jack Torrance's insane novel, a sign that he will soon attempt filicide, in which the same sentence, "All work and no play makes Jack a dull boy," is written over and over, for hundreds of pages.)

Uncanny moments occurred all the time in Angus's classes: moments that felt both familiar and strange, inevitable and weird, "of course" and "what the fuck?" One early autumn day, referring to his famous book *Allegory*, Angus observed that characters who take their identities from conventional symbols, like crosses or roses or serpents, are *daemonic*. They are driven by an uncontrollable inner force to behave in one way: the cross character must behave charitably, the rosy one is devoted to romantic love, and the serpentine guy is pernicious. Then Angus said, roughly: "But then how are we to know if we ourselves are not acting out an allegorical plot not of our own making, if your so-called leading virtue, charity or charisma, say, isn't something you've cultivated and now control but the other way around: your virtue is controlling and cultivating you, as Socrates's daemon did him, by reminding him almost daily of his main purpose in life, *gnothi seauton*, know thyself?" I thought, "There is no way of knowing," and was afraid to turn my head, lift my hand. What if every time I believed I was moving, something, something foreign, monstrous, was moving me?

Another time: it was the Wednesday before Thanksgiving, when everyone in the department, except for those of us in Angus's class and Angus, had left for the holiday and it felt as if we were the last of the Overlook Hotel's close-down crew in Kubrick's horror movie, the remnant that prepares for emptiness. On this day, Angus brought in a copy of some tabloid he had whimsically purchased from a newsstand on his way from the subway station to the Grad Center, then in the Grace Building on Forty-second Street. On the cover was a cloud formation resembling a giant demon—Cumulus Lucifer, I would have said, had I not been so shy and afraid of appearing, before Angus and the other grad students, to be *daft*. The headline read SATAN APPEARS IN CLOUD. Angus said, "I saw this and wondered, 'What does it mean, to *appear*?'" Yes, I thought. Think of how we use the verb "appear." A ghost *appears*. A celebrity *appears*. A relative, though, *shows up*. And I, when entering a room, *enter*, just as I, attending a party, *attend*.

Remarks like these made me hyperattentive to everything Angus said. I didn't know when he might, like a Zen master, utter some koanesque phrase that would alter, as might a pair of colored glasses, everything I thereafter witnessed. And so, on that very day before Thanksgiving, just as we were shuffling out of class, Angus said, "Well, once a friend of mine told me that if you're going to cook a turkey, just put it in the oven and leave it in there for four hours and it will be cooked." Was this just a bland description of what happens when you cook a turkey or a deep statement on the nature of existence?

I believe that Angus's otherworldly qualities—were *they* controlling *him*?—were enhanced by his clothing choices: old black Chuck Taylors, duct-taped around the toes, apparently because they leaked; equally old khaki pants; a gray L.L. Bean–type crewneck; horn-rimmed glasses; wild gray hair, as if he had just put his hands on one of those electrified globes that junior high science teachers use to exemplify the behavior of static electricity and to make their volunteers suffer the indignity of having their hair raised, as if they were hanging upside down. If he were wearing a soiled, rumpled lab coat, I would say he fringed the genotype mad scientist. If his memory weren't so voluminous, I would call him an absentminded professor. Since he was so insanely intricate and disorienting, idea-wise, and so mnemonically profound, his mind opening into compartment after compartment of ancient and modern books, I did call him, not to his face, *labyrinthine.*

The idea of something—a concept, a state of mind, a place—being labyrinthine fascinated Angus. He wrote about the labyrinth as a state or space of bewilderment in his book on Edmund Spenser, *The Prophetic Moment,* in which the confusing maze is contrasted with the temple, place of tranquillity and clarity. In that book, and in other works, like his riveting essay titled "'Positive Negation': Threshold, Sequence, and Personification in Coleridge" (which inspired me to write *Coleridge's Melancholia: An Anatomy of Limbo*), Angus is most interested in the boundary between temple and labyrinth and how it feels to cross it, one direction or the other. Angus, if anything, as another professor put it, was "liminal," attuned to what happens at the threshold.

Lo and behold, I've just come across a rare piece of Fletcherania, on the home page of an Italian poet, playwright, and essayist named Nanni Cagnone. In 1979, back when Angus looked something, if the photo on the page is accurate, like a cross between John Berryman, sans biblical beard, and Iggy Pop, pre–*Dead Man*, and Neil Young, *Tonight's the Night* phase (c. 1975, exactly twenty years before Neil composed the sound track to Jarmusch's *Dead Man*), Angus wrote a little review of Cagnone's collection *What's Hecuba to Him or He to Hecuba?*, which I am totally getting, even if it costs $27.50 used on Amazon .com and has a sales rank, by *far* the lowest I've ever seen, of

11,209,648 (compared with which, the 359,971 rank of my latest appears to be a bestseller). In that piece, you can get a feel for Angus at his most playful, writing about, yes, a labyrinth, in connection to the temple, and the space in between: "The threshold does not exist; it is fairly pure betweenness. So you swing with das Zwischen. (Note on 'error,' from Ariosto and others, eg. [*sic*] Spenser: *errare*, wandering knights, planets, maze-walking: varieties of maze, mountains, the Grand Canyon [*sic*] vs Bryce Canyon—or Zion—in the State of Utah, the maze at Hampton Court; Olivier and Michael Caine; Marvell's 'Garden,' William Empson on 'complex words,' etc.)."

I'll leave this cryptic litany alone, except to say, Olivier and Caine played in a 1972 film titled *Sleuth*, which featured a hedge maze (built for the film on the grounds at Athelhampton House in Dorset), and Caine once owned a pub near the Hampton Court hedge maze, located near London.

So. After my first class with Angus, I wanted to *be* Angus, to be labyrinthine. I was already, by this time, well on my way to "weirding" the Larry Darrell persona I had created in college: studious, serious, diligent, regular, hungry only for the A. From the minute I moved from Boone to New York, I started drafting a new script, titled "The Country Boy moves to the Big City." To make good among the skyscrapers, I felt I needed to drop my Southern accent—diphthongs be gone—as well as expunge Southern colloquialisms (except for, when someone runs fast, "He took out of there like a scalded dog") and ingrained grammatical errors (like "might could"). I also did the exact opposite of what I imagined my rural townsfolk doing and so became liberal, wine-drunk, ironic, neurotic, androgynous with a capital "David Bowie." I moreover actually got educated, seriously. I read ferociously, from Homer to Seamus Heaney, desperate to make up for a fifth-rate junior high and high school education and an only slightly better than average college one.

(Now, wiser and sadder, I feel about so-called intellectuals, especially academics, English professors in particular, almost the same way I once felt about my rural townsfolk: that I can't get far enough away. At least, I have come to learn, there was among my fellow country dwellers an engaging suspicion of pomposity, a strange verbal lyricism [such as, in telling a boy to rush to school, "Break brush over to the state high school"], a physical vigor, and the deep lonesomeness of Celtic immigrants, who sense "I shouldn't really be here." I know this all sounds as if I'm romanticizing rural life, as I once idealized the city, and I probably am.)

Very soon after arriving in NYC, I had almost perfected my act. Other students in my Ph.D. program asked me where I was from, barely able to detect my Southern accent. They admired, or seemed to admire, my left-leaning pose, bolstered with highbrow allusions to William Blake, Oscar Wilde, Theodor Adorno, Zora Neale Hurston, Herbert Marcuse, Langston Hughes, Jean-Paul Sartre, Henri Lefebvre, Maya Angelou, Abbie Hoffman, Allen Ginsberg, and Noam Chomsky. They also apparently were impressed with my knowledge of French theory—Derrida, Lacan, Foucault—and the Continental philosophers from whom it emerged: Friedrich Nietzsche, Martin Heidegger, and Hans-Georg Gadamer. The ostensible proof of my critical and literary acuteness: I had been awarded one of a handful of teaching fellowships.

Eventually, I found my way to Angus Fletcher's seminar and saw how boring my antirural persona was. I had become a caricature of "hip grad student": blue jeans, Doc Martens, black blazer, black T-shirts, little round John Lennon glasses, long early-Bono-style hair, invoking the Frankfurt School like word-magic. Then Angus appeared and in an instant, with one uncanny sentence, or two, made me feel reductive, obvious, ridiculous. What to do? Gather more French theoretical odds and ends and purchase more black clothing? Return to the just-out-of-overalls cornpone, play up William Styron's–Stingo's ingenue? No. Be like Angus. *Labyrinthine.*

Which meant, to me, lacking Angus's cerebral capaciousness and Hamlet-like wit, simply trying to be oddball, substituting blunt peculiarity for unsettling subtlety, H. P. Lovecraft, say, for Edgar Allan Poe, or Carl Solomon for Franz Kafka, not that I could touch, if there were garments on H.P. or C.S., the hems. My new role (still, alas, somewhat in progress, though I'm in the process of abandoning it) involved such studied idiosyncrasies as wearing brown Timberland boots, houndstooth blazers, and flannel shirts (a "RetroJethro" look); cultivating a weird tale interest, devoted to, in addition to Lovecraft, Lord Dunsany, Algernon Blackwood (still love "The Man Whom the Trees Loved"), and Arthur Machen, whose *The Great God Pan*, if read enough times, might transport a man, for real, into a realm of myth and purposelessness; citing the periodic table of elements as a major influence on my self-fashioned "object poetry," poems containing only nouns; espousing the idea that a weeklong study of the Weather Channel could be the basis for many a tenure-worthy monograph; spending Friday afternoons walking from Hell's Kitchen down to SoHo, drinking from a forty-ounce beer, held in a paper bag, and slipping, flaneur desirous, into reveries of the fin de siècle; and citing seemingly inexplicable pop song lyrics as sites of unwittingly defamiliarizing surrealism that startle listeners into sudden awarenesses of the earth's untrammeledness, e.g., "skip the light fandango" (Procol Harum's "Whiter Shade of Pale"), "Revved up like a deuce, another runner in the night" (Manfred Mann's Earth Band's "Blinded by the Light," a cover of Bruce Springsteen's original, which says "cut loose like a deuce," referring, rather unambiguously, to the slang for a 1932 Ford coupé), "rocket man, burning out his fuse up here alone" (Elton John's, or Reginald Kenneth Dwight's, "Rocket Man")—none of which should be confused with mondegreens, mishearings as a result of homophony, as in John/Dwight's "Hold me closer, tiny dancer," sounding like "Hold me closer, Tony Danza."

You can say: "Man, that's pitiful, an immature effort to escape from what you saw as the limitations of your upbringing and to pretend to be something you're not. If you had any integrity, you would have acknowledged that your childhood made you who you are today, giving you as many virtues as vices, and you would have embraced your past, been true to it."

You can say that. You can say it again when you hear that my trying to be labyrinthine opened me to a deeper appreciation of my past, an appreciation that invigorated my present and energized my future. For what is the desire to be labyrinthine but a hope to be, one day, an angel?

So suggests Robert Hass in his introduction to the poems of Rainer Maria Rilke, where he explores those moments "whenever our souls make us strangers to the world," moments that occur when "children [are] at home by themselves looking in the mirror . . . lovers [are] bewildered by the intensity of their feelings . . . solitaries [are] out walking after dinner." All of us know such instances and the impulse that follows from them: "to imagine that we were meant to be citizens of some other place. It is from this sensation that the angels come into existence, creating in this world their ambience of pure loss."

38.

Trying to be the boy who didn't first say "ball" by going disco for a day: this was a fine, fleeting game, revealing to me a panache I didn't know I possessed, but that I didn't really build upon until much later. How much of a role that day played in my love of Oscar Wilde and Charles Baudelaire and Walter Benjamin, great lovers of artifice and city walking, and in my own urban dandyism, I don't know, but like to think that it, Travolta for an hour, or three, was more than a walk-on, at least a line or two and an end credit.

My next great role, as Bill Murray's Larry Darrell: this was a richer part, much more complicated and durable and deliberate. I chose to don the mask of Murray Darrell, and it, this artifice, made me more Wilson, empowering me to explore intellectual and artistic passions that before had garnered only a cursory glance, as well as inspiring me to foster new intensities: for scholarship and traveling and writing.

When the zig simply darts from the zag, eventually the difference between the two disappears: In the zigzag, who knows or cares which angle is which? My Darrell act became as predictable and one-dimensional and stilted as the jock with a slight flair for glam. I realized this soon after moving to New York City, and I longed for the labyrinth, a geometry comprising multitudinous zigs and zags alike: manifold, baroque and bewildering, symmetrical and surprising at once, where the familiar (perfectly squared turns) becomes crazed (fuck! a Minotaur) and the bizarre (that half man/half beast of nightmare) is ultimately meaningful (yes, I can tame, like Theseus, my own animal within).

I committed to the uncanny, the melancholy, the traumatic, the outlandish, the sublime, terrae incognitae, a devotion that eventually inspired a whole career of intellectual work, including books on Coleridge's melancholia, the outré geographies of the North and South Poles, the emotions of androids, David Lynch's strange worlds, the cultural history of sorrow, and William Blake's disturbing apocalypse.

This faith in the more bewildering parts of experience granted me another gift: a nourishing affinity for the gothic arts, ranging from Coleridge's poetry to the engravings of Albrecht Dürer to the paintings of Matthias Grünewald to Stanley Kubrick's cinema to the music of Dock Boggs, Buell Kazee, Clarence Ashley, and Bascom Lamar Lunsford.

Through the haunted music of these Appalachian singers, I saw my own mountain heritage afresh, spreading on my father's side from the early nineteenth century onward, when the Wilsons and Womacks emigrated from the Hibernian borderlands to the Blue Ridges of Buncombe and McDowell counties. In the holler where my kin lived were hard-drinking great-uncles who turned harder ministers; cousins venting their pains in shotgun blasts; men whose family relation was unclear, smoking themselves to death, and their wives, who dipped snuff and spit brown into Prince Albert tobacco tins; frenzied humor, less spoken than jerked; houses abandoned by millworkers; old scraps of canvas and metal left in these houses; a cold cave where there were arrowheads; rooms whose white ceilings were stained in greasy black; wintergreen odor on blue cotton work shirts; loam on hands and boots; hog blood; frying animal fat; folks who stare at you as if you were not there.

I admit that I romanticized the poverty and struggle of my mountain relatives, but this skewed vision nonetheless allowed me to see my father in a fuller, more meaningful context, not simply as the football coach who wanted his boy to say "ball" but as a man burdened with humility bordering on shame and harried by a drive to get clean and win and be at home in the world. I saw this new father in myself and felt for the first time in my life the weird goad of failure, suspecting that I could never win and get cleansed enough, but the falling short would be more compelling—I didn't know why—than the having of victory.

39.

"Art is the lie that enables us to realize the truth": Pablo Picasso. Camus: "Fiction is the lie through which we tell the truth." "Man is least himself when he talks in his own person. Give him a mask, and he will tell you the truth," from Oscar Wilde. All of which is to explain this: in 2009 a *Time* magazine poll showed that Jon Stewart is the most trusted newscaster in America, post-Cronkite. Stewart is of course the anchor of Comedy Central's *The Daily Show*, a fake news show devoted to the satire of mainstream journalism, mainly with an eye toward exposing hypocrisy in politicians. Of those polled, 44 percent hailed Stewart as trustworthy, a percentage easily higher than those garnered by the newscasters from the three major television networks, Brian Williams, Katie Couric, and Charlie Gibson. (I imagine that no newscaster from the fourth significant network, Fox, was even worth considering as trustworthy.) In 2004 another poll, this one from the Pew Research Center, found that 21 percent of the eighteen to twenty-nine demographic tuned into satire-based news shows such as Stewart's *The Daily Show* and *SNL* to get their actual news, a number that nearly equals the 23 percent that went to more traditional sources for their information. This younger 21 percent isn't stupid, another Pew Research poll, from April 15, 2007, suggests. According to this latter poll, 54 percent of those who watched Stewart's show as well as Stephen Colbert's similarly satirical show, *The Colbert Report*, demonstrated a high knowledge of current events, in both national and international arenas. Surprisingly, these viewers, the poll further proved, were more knowledgeable than those who regularly watched PBS's *The News Hour with Jim Lehrer*.

The reasons for these numbers aren't hard to find. Stewart appears to be politically unaffiliated, whereas mainstream news shows betray ideological commitments. While Fox expresses an obvious conservative bias, CBS, ABC, and NBC seem to lean slightly to the left. Mocking Democrats and Republicans with equal gusto, Stewart comes across as objective. Moreover, as I've already mentioned, Stewart focuses on the hypocrisy of politicians, often by revealing contradictions in their speeches and interviews. Uncovering lies, again, with apparently no agenda to push, Stewart *presents* as truthful. Finally, in acknowledging that his news is fake—that is, unconcerned with prioritizing important stories, journalistic integrity, and accuracy in reporting—Stewart seems to be admitting what most of us suspect to be true of all mainstream journalism anyway: that it, too, is fake. In a world in which almost everyone is lying but trying to pass his lies off as truth, the man who confesses he is lying becomes, ironically, a teller of truth.

The formula again emerges: to believe that you're authentic in a world where nothing is authentic but performed is inauthentic; to know that you're inauthentic in a world in which nothing is not performed is authentic. So if you behave as if you're actually authentic, then you are a liar, and if you comport yourself with an awareness of your inauthenticity, you are as real as it gets.

The poet Wallace Stevens agrees: "The final belief is to believe in a fiction, which you know to be a fiction, there being nothing else. The exquisite truth is to know that it is a fiction and that you believe in it willingly." But what fiction do you believe? Are all fictions the same?

No. For Stevens, two forces contend in the world: reality and imagination. Reality is everything that makes us fail: the senseless, painful, deadly. Imagination can counter, transforming opportunity into success, nonsense into meaning, suffering into wisdom, death into the stark limit goading us to explore our potentials.

Hamlet—glimmering in his melancholy, his mind capacious as St. Peter's Basilica and more baroque, his wit close to Oscar Wilde's, as good-looking as a young Ralph Fiennes, as morally sophisticated as Aristotle—gets murdered by Laertes, the vengeful moron. Excellent men are killed by idiots. This distresses us. Horatio, Hamlet's faithful friend, holds his dead companion, solacing us: "Now cracks a noble heart. Good night, sweet prince: / And flights of angels sing thee to thy rest!" Demise is muse, raises corpse to sainthood, hurt to contemplation, and nears the heavenly spheres' music; angel song accompanies; and all is undying sweetness and light.

But it's all fiction, these intoning angels and the eternity that is their bliss. Fiction, but no less true—in fact, the truest, when the most beautiful. Does it matter if what Horatio says is true, if his words explain, organize, enliven, nourish, make life livable? Without such art—meaning-making miracle, heart-resonant, to higher vibrations humming—loss and pain, pain and loss, no recovery, no redemption, nothing.

Or, as a friend of mine once pronounced, in the middle of a long hike in the Blue Ridge Mountains: "It's all illusion, man; choose your own well." (He also said, "That's cow shit you've got on your Vasques there.")

40.

My friend was a consummate English major and so had read Woolf's *To the Lighthouse* and might well have based his pithy apothegm on this book on the power of artifice, though the Guns N' Roses album *Use Your Illusion* is a more likely source. In this novel, Woolf in her famous "Time Passes" chapter describes how time inevitably destroys all human order: houses, histories, husbands, children. Just before this chapter is a scene in which several of Mrs. Ramsay's children and the guests she and Mr. Ramsay have invited to their summer home in the Hebrides all return from a satisfying evening by the seaside. Entering the house, "smoothly brushing the walls, they passed on musingly as if asking the red and yellow roses on the wallpaper whether they would fade, and questioning (gently, for there was time at their disposal) the torn letters in the wastepaper basket, the flowers, the books, all of which were now open to them and asking, Were they allies? Were they enemies? How long would they endure?"

This brief meditation on endurance leads into one of the most brutal and moving ten or so pages in literature, in the course of which we watch the Scottish weather attack relentlessly and rapidly deteriorate the house, while tragedy ravages the former inhabitants, worlds away, each death rendered by Woolf, shockingly, within brackets, suggesting the insignificance of these lives we've come to value so highly in the book's opening one-hundred-odd pages. Andrew, one of the Ramsay children, is blown up by a shell in the First World War. Prue, another, dies in childbirth. Most disturbingly, Mrs. Ramsay, into whose complex, glittering, compassionate, vulnerable, insecure, beauty-loving consciousness we have been, paragraph by lyrical paragraph, streamed, dies suddenly one night, leaving her husband "stumbling along a passage one dark morning," his arms stretched out, but remaining "empty."

Woolf's novel wails with such startlingly sorrowful moments, when the inhuman and gargantuan gales of time devastate all that is significant to us, all that we love. The book asserts over and over again that the world minus human awareness is meaningless, stupid. The sea, for instance, "like a ghostly roll of drums remorselessly beat[s] the measure of life, [makes] one think [as it does in this case the still-living Mrs. Ramsay] of the destruction of the island and its engulfment in the sea," and warns that each day slips "past in one quick doing after another," "that it [is] all ephemeral as a rainbow." To the woman desperate to love her life—her family, her home, her beauty—the ocean thunders horrifically, drowning her heart's tiny beats.

How to counter the entropy? Create brief orders that seem to calm the heartless groan. Only seconds before Mrs. Ramsay falls into her terrible reverie, the distant murmur of men's voices—they are likely talking philosophy—and the "taking out of pipes and the putting in of pipes," and "the tap of balls upon bats, the sharp, sudden bark now and then, 'How's that?

How's that?' of the children playing cricket": these sounds intermingle with the surf's gratings to compose "a measured and soothing tattoo to her thoughts," a beat that "consolingly" repeats, morphs, in her ears, to "the words of some old cradle song, murmured by nature, 'I am guarding you—I am your support.'"

The ear, our body's innate artist, wields the hammer, tiptaps the anvil, turns, without trying, the monotonous slammings of water and sand into sweet rockabyes. Fairly flat art. Anyone can do it.

A more powerful structuring: the domestic order, not "highly conscious" but forceful, later established by Mrs. McNab and Mrs. Bast, the cleaning ladies who, though old and stiff, scrub and organize the Ramsays' home on the Isle of Skye, after it has descended into filth and disrepair, ravaged by the "fertility, the insensibility of nature."

But almost anyone can of course accomplish such housework if she has moderate vim and fortitude. There are yet higher orders, if "higher" here means heightened possibility, complexity, ability to transform not buildings without but those inner architectures, call them emotions, thoughts, imaginings, temperaments. Here think of the game of cricket, blind motion subdued by rules, themselves made exciting and graceful by the playing. Who knows who will win, what records might be set, what efforts, Herculean and blithe, might rise into beauty and remain as jewels in our running-down hearts? Brood also on the conversation, sound waves rounded and whistled and stopped and released into semantics, grammar, syntax, rhetoric, forms admitting an almost infinite variety of expression and communication.

Still other orders, necessitating even more skill and scope:

the cooking of the famous *boeuf en daube*, the main dish of a dinner party on Skye, presided nervously over by the consummate hostess Mrs. Ramsay, who, until the platter of tender, warm beef arrives, frets over the awkward silences, the forced talk, the whole affair teetering on failure, but then finds herself gathered into ecstasy when the sustenance arrives in the candlelight perfectly executed, holding everyone's expectation and delight, everyone now unified in his or her crepuscular beauty—the candles make all faces interesting—and in her or his appreciation of the beautiful dish, everyone drawn into an abrupt harmony, as intricate and compelling as a group dance.

Cooking is an art, but an ephemeral one, constrained to raw flesh and fruits rushing toward rot, to appetites that come and go, to heartburn and gas, to fire that will not burn forever. Fine art, poetry or musical composition or painting, is different. It requires more talent than does cooking, or carpentry, because it, the art, needs, in ways that more expedient crafts do not, intelligence, imagination, empathy, insight, courage, weirdness, nonconformity, freedom, as well as extremely refined, and often well-trained, technical prowess.

In the novel, Lily Briscoe, a summer visitor to the Ramsay island home, exemplifies the force of fine art, even though she is far from a brilliant and accomplished painter. An amateur, she struggles over the course of the book to paint Mrs. Ramsay reading to her son James, as she saw them one afternoon through the cottage window, from her vantage point outside on the lawn. For her, this moment stands out from others, is especially luminous, evocative, dense, significant.

It is such a memory as another one she possesses, of playing on the beach with the other visitors while Mrs. Ramsay sits by and watches. This recollection, a "moment of friend-ship and liking," has stayed in her mind, "affecting [her] al-most like a work of art." Such moments as these are the "little daily miracles, illuminations, matches struck unexpectedly in the dark" that give life its meaning, intensity, textures. They inspire one to say, "Life stand still here," in hopes of "making of the moment something permanent."

These "moments of being," Woolf called them elsewhere, assure us that "in the midst of chaos there [is] shape," that this "eternal passing and flowing" can sometimes be "struck into stability." To render such moments artistically is a high and useful calling, preserving these refulgent instances in endur-ing, engrossing form. This is Lily's task, to elevate the after-noon Mrs. Ramsay read to James into a long-lasting structure, there for her to behold and cherish and gain vivification from for decades. This is what she achieves, at novel's end finishing her painting, on which she has worked off and on for over ten years—completing the picture and, upon "laying down her brush in extreme fatigue," concluding: "I have had my vision."

Amateur paintings, photography, poems and such: all these intone to certain moments, *Be still*, and archive them for ongoing gazing and delight, providing a feeling to those scrap-booking or looking or whatnot that there *are* meaningful peri-ods, periods more real than others—more fascinating, more precious, more vital—and that these durations are about as real as it gets. What, then, of the greatest artists, the Woolfs and the Beethovens and the Turners?

To describe what constitutes the greatest art is impossible, and only an idiot tries to do it with rigor. Hint, gist, sugges-tion are best, and the assumption that we all, if it came down to it, would agree that the works of Virginia Woolf, Ludwig van Beethoven, and Joseph Turner share these glories: stillness and permanence—an ocean-cliff calm and lastingness; quick darts of thought and emotion, as unpredictable as silvery eels; giant scope, solving mysteries or revealing the unsolvable, from the depths of the darkest fin to the star-high firmament; complexity, depicting life's bewilderingly intricate anatomies; and simplicity, in the midst of the crazed paradoxes, reminding us that this is *it*, now, here, always, and nothing you can do about it, and everything.

41.

You are a nucleus in an atom, a regular patterning of blind force, a whirl and a whirl and a whirl, turning, turning, the livelong day, dull round, dull round, the same goddamn dull round. What's your story, subatomic core? An old one: you are a cog in a massive machine, repeating the same action over and over, lacking agency and creativity, compelled by a "have to" you've obeyed so long that you've forgotten it exists.

You are a cell in a carp, a fish big as a piglet and mud-loving too, being a bottom-feeder. You're bigger than the atoms that compose you, and more sensitive, reacting more subtly to your environment of fishy guts and blood than a yeoman nucleus does to the electromagnetic fields that set and keep it spinning. A hook pierces the flesh near where you quiver; you rush to heal it. Your finny fellow sucks up a toxin; you flag in energy, until he digests that poison and sends it turdward. Yes, cell, you are animate and so capable of a wider range of experiences than atoms and open to more changes and more chance.

You're the carp itself now, getting bigger every day, approaching now, a wide-eyed boy would say if you were caught, sowhood. You're still low on the choice-making, being driven by instinct—eat and fuck, eat and fuck, and sleep, if fish sleep—but your life is by far more varied than that cell in your belly or that atom in the cell, and so . . . well, your narrative is more interesting, varied, complicated, and so . . . well, I can't go up the entire chain of being here, like the author (Rose Bonne) of "I Know an Old Lady Who Swallowed a Fly" kind of did in a very disturbing way, depicting some crazed geriatric swallowing a fly, no one knows why, and then consuming increasingly larger animals to eat the vermin, until she chomps a horse, which—deservedly, I believe—kills her.

Still, you're an otter. You can eat a fucking carp, I guess. You can put your head above water, look around, or go under. You can pat your belly. You can live in a zoo. You can have stuffed versions of you made, and key chains, on which dangle tiny plastic versions of you that my daughter, who unaccountably collects key chains though she has no keys, buys.

You're a human, and you can swim, and you can kill the otter with a club or look at it and say, "How *cute*," and you can catch the carp with a nasty-looking hook—three-pronged—and you can say "gross" to all water not chlorinated, and you can say, "I wish to hell I were out of this stinky water."

You're a human. Yes. You can build a boat and sail to the muddy bank, like the one Thoreau witnessed long ago, oozing its springtime muck-melt into lobes and globes, letters and leaves. Yes, and you can also jog away from water, take a shower, and get a job and buy a car and drive to the desert, where there are lizards, big and sage green and long-tongued. You can fly in a plane, too, if you so desire, to Las Vegas. You can fly in another plane, at least part of the way, to Venice, before having to sail in another boat, over waters lacking carp, far as I know.

Step on those stones of Venice, think, with John Ruskin, that it, Venice, "is the Paradise of cities and there is a *moon* enough to make half the sanities of earth *lunatic*." You can rocket to the moon one day. Put aside your Ruskin volume first, though, because he was loony when it came to the pubis, believing before his marriage to a woman named Effie that all vaginas looked like those of classical art's hairless nudes and growing so horrified when he witnessed Effie's wedding night mound that he rejected her and soon after had the marriage annulled. You're flying to the moon, dreaming of Saturn's rings, and of the book of Sebald on the melancholy sphere's girdles, and of the picture in that book, early on (picture black and white ghostly, not needing photo-shop sepia for its timelessness), of the skull of Sir Thomas Browne, the seventeenth-century physician from Norwich, home, later, of Pender's knockabout comedians, the acrobatic group Archie Leach joined and through whose auspices he sailed to America to become Cary, and you recall Browne's uncanny tractates on buried urns and quincunxes, and his broodings on how earth is too evanescent to feel at all real:

And therefore restless inquietude for the diuturnity of our memories unto present considerations seems a vanity almost out of date and superannuated piece of folly. We cannot hope to live so long in our names, as some have done in their persons; one face of Janus holds no proportion unto the other. 'Tis too late to be ambitious. The great mutations of the world are acted, or time may be too short for our designs. To extend our memories by monuments, whose death we daily pray for, and whose duration we cannot hope without injury to our expectations in the advent of the last day, were a contradiction to our beliefs. We whose generations are ordained in this setting part of time, are providentially taken off from such imaginations. And being necessitated to eye the remaining particle of futurity, are naturally constituted unto thoughts of the next world, and cannot excusably decline the consideration of that duration, which maketh pyramids pillars of snow, and all that's past a moment.

My parable has now passed, atoms up to urn anatomies, hoping to symbolize different grades of fiction-making, fictions here being the narratives we can choose for organizing and making meaningful life. For Debord and Co., most of us, by global capitalism seduced, are little better than atoms when it comes to intensity of consciousness, ability to think critically and creatively, quantity and quality of choices. Like atoms, we unconsciously follow in the footsteps of the consuming masses, believing we're free, when really we are just players in a spectacle arranged and produced by faceless, indifferent promoters, deploying us to fill their pockets.

Others might feel in their atomhood the splinter in the mind, such as Keanu Reeves's incipient Neo felt in *The Matrix* I, the sense that what appears to be real isn't really real. These might start to question the narrative into which their society has thrown them, labor to create their own stories, more suitable to their potentials. Of course, the media powers of capitalism are sly and can contain such rebellions.

Just look, again, at Neo. He rebels against mechanisms that reduce our lives to images we take for reality, much in the same way that one of us might rebel against scripts by which the ruling ideology flattens us to predictable spectacles. But Neo is simply performing the *conventions* of rebellion, mimicking hundreds of other cinematic bad boys, going back to Dean and Brando, themselves going back (though they surely don't know it, not being, as far as I know, serious poetry readers) to Rimbaud, who was begat by Byron, Hamlet-spawned, and so on, all the way back to Cain, who was the first, tradition has it, gnostic hero, breaking the rules of an oppressive deity the only way he knew how, raising questions about this God's power and spreading discord. But what if this God, though far from the best (who would fashion a world in which people suffer and evil thrives?), is actually in control all the while, letting us and Cain and Neo believe we can challenge him, when he's watching us from above as if we were tired lightning bugs trapped in a Mason jar, only three holes, screwdriver-poked, through which to breathe?

So, to return to my parable, carp-cell types—carps themselves, pond swimmers—even skilled fishermen, all who question the standard and attempt to fashion their own: these might still be simply enacting prefabricated narratives, flattening themselves to nothing more than clichés, and therefore supporting the system they, the rebels, profess to hate.

As consciousness and creativity increase, narratives become more complicated, more open, and, we hope, more challenging to the master narratives forged by those in power. The makers of these plots, the philosophers and artists and poets, are, yes, the road trippers, the jet-setters, the space travelers, gaining wide and varied vistas, enjoying an infinite number of possibilities for motion, intellectual and physical. Woolf would be orbiting Saturn, if she wanted; Turner, drifting, at his pleasure, with the stratosphere; Beethoven, tuning his by-God ear to the music, almost solely angel-heard, of the spheres.

"The eye is the first circle," Emerson writes. "The horizon

which it forms is the second; and throughout nature this primary figure is repeated without end," with each new thought composing a new circle, wider than and containing those coming before it. Just as the nucleus is at the center of the atom, with each larger orbit whirling concentrically around it, including and surpassing in complexity and capacity the smaller one preceding, so the eye of a person, like a pebble dropped into a pond, emanates outward its interpretive horizons, the most powerful visions proving the most potent stones, generating strong and multitudinous ripples.

And where do you undulate, fellow artist? As if you could be anything but an artist, once you think or speak, a meaning-making creature. And me. Am I in the carp's gut, turning, or touring in the millionth Apollo?

42.

I have a good friend named John McElwee. He has published an excellent book titled *Showmen, Sell It Hot!: Movies as Merchandise in Golden Era Hollywood*. Along with my addictions to Cary Grant and Bill Murray, this story he told me is as much a reason for writing *Keep It Fake* as any other.

When John was in college, he fell in with an avid movie collector known as Moon Mullin. By then an elderly man, Moon had for most of his life been accumulating 16mm film prints. A lover of classic movies and an aspiring film collector himself, John heard about Moon from the small subculture of cinema buffs living in the town where he went to college. He soon latched onto Moon as a mentor. At a time when most old films were still protected by copyright and studios were urging the FBI to prosecute individuals owning copyrighted films, movie collecting was a largely underground and somewhat dangerous activity. Indifferent to the risk and keen for a pristine print of *The Wolf Man*, *Earth vs. the Flying Saucers*, or *Red River*, John enthusiastically entered Moon's obscure world of celluloid intrigue. Within weeks of their first meeting, John was cutting classes to take excursions to condemned movie houses and backwoods barns, dank basements and rusted warehouses. He was on a fevered quest to recover the lost Edens of the Saturday matinee: the silvery cowboys on the prairie, sci-fi creatures untroubled by time, the dream-tortured monsters of horror.

One such journey took place in winter. Moon told John that he had heard of a man deep in the Blue Ridge Mountains of North Carolina who owned an immense cache of old Hollywood movies and memorabilia. It was a snowy Thursday, and the roads were treacherously slick and curvy. After almost sliding off the highway into a ravine, John pulled over and refused to go farther. Moon, however, told him that he would guide him. John pushed ahead through the blinding whiteness, listening to Moon's advice on steering and speed. Finally, they reached their destination, a shabby mobile home decaying in front of a huge, freshly painted red barn. They knocked on the door of the trailer. An old man wearing white pajamas and a black bathrobe appeared. His greasy hair was combed back like Bela Lugosi's in *Dracula*. Through rheumy eyes, he stared at John and Moon as if they were from another world. When Moon asked if he had any movies, the man led them to the barn. It was brimming with silver film canisters.

John can't remember the old man's name. What Moon purchased has also slipped his mind. What he does recall is that he soon found an original print of a Raoul Walsh western from 1948, *Silver River*, starring an aging Errol Flynn.

Before buying, John asked to watch a clip. The old man wordlessly walked out of the barn and into the falling snow. John followed. He saw at the edge of the woods a small building little bigger than an outhouse, a makeshift projectionist booth. Inside was a polished 35mm projector. While the old man threaded the film, John looked for where the movie would appear. The projector was aimed at the forest. The old man had hewed a swath through which the light could travel. At the end of this treeless corridor was a large white screen. It hovered in the falling snow like a phantom.

A beam of light streamed out of the booth, flowing through the flakes. There at the edge of the snowy woods in the hour of twilight, miles from another living soul: Errol Flynn in striking black and white. A Saturday movie house bloomed in the wild. Nineteen-year-old John became a child again, too confused by wonder to think of the disjointed miracle of the scene, of the sixty dollars he would soon pay for the film, of the fact that the snow was already turning to slush.

43.

When I saw *Blue Velvet* in the fall of 1986—in a little second-run theater in Hickory, Boone, or Charlotte—I was astounded. So a film, I asked (really, *asserted*) can do *that*? Kyle MacLachlan's Jeffrey hides in the closet of a strange woman he doesn't know, Isabella Rossellini's Dorothy. He is playing amateur sleuth, purely out of gee-whiz kid curiosity. He watches Dorothy, who knows he is hiding in the closet, get raped—a transgression she appears to like as much as loathe—by Dennis Hopper's Frank Booth. During the assault, Frank beats Dorothy, commands her to do things as a general would a soldier ("Don't you fuckin' look at me!"), falls into the role of a child ("Baby wants to fuck"), chews on part of Dorothy's blue velvet robe, violently inhales amyl nitrate, and intimates—all the while, remember, Jeffrey is, unbeknownst to him, playing the voyeur—that he has kidnapped her husband and son. He has already cut off the husband's ear as a warning to her not to call the police—an ear Jeffrey discovered in a field near his home and that pulled him into this mystery in the first place.

But such scenes were only the beginning of my astonishment. There was the tone, rivetingly ambiguous, by turns deadly earnest, as with the rape scene, and patently silly, as when Jeffrey and his high school teenybopper girlfriend Sandy (Laura Dern) fall into *Happy Days* badinage in the local soda shop. Usually, though, the tone was a mixture of the ridiculous and the serious. Sandy reports to Jeffrey, rapturously, her dream of robins who can redeem the wasted land, and he responds, sheepishly, "You're a neat girl." At the film's conclusion, an obviously mechanical robin chews on a seemingly real worm on the windowsill of Jeffrey's family's kitchen; Jeffrey and Sandy recall cheesily the dream and smile at each other with more treacle in their teeth than prebrush plaque.

And more, I was stunned by the film's visuals. Highly saturated depictions of flowers and sky, straight out of fifties Technicolor TV, with surreal subterranean visions of teeming glistening insects, viciously crunching and clicking. The entre-deux-guerres Berlinesque cabaret scenes, in which Dorothy as the Blue Lady croons into luridly gorgeous bluish light. Disturbing yet beautiful interiors, as in Dorothy's dreamily sordid Deep River apartment, with its mauve carpet, black-and-white tile, purplish burgundy walls, and lime green radiator and plant pots. An opening sequence in which a floor-to-ceiling blue velvet curtain slowly waves in muted light, to the rhythm of Angelo Badalamenti's ghoulish score, in such a way that it looks as though the cloth were alive.

And finally, I had never seen a film using such strange music throughout, not only Badalamenti's outré sequences, worthy of the opera's Phantom, but also Roy Orbison's "In Dreams," which Dean Stockwell's character, Ben, lip-syncs into a portable lightbulb, while wearing makeup and suavely dressed in a suit redolent of Lord Byron, with ruffled collar and jacket of satin, printed into swirls of black and gold.

What tantalized me most in each of these cinematic elements was *doubleness*, the picture's ability to be stupid and sublime at once, inspiring at the same time tears and laughter. I now realize that this quality—let's call it, along with David Foster Wallace, Lynchian—is common to all of Lynch's great films, which means *all* of his films, except *Dune* (his only film on which he didn't have final cut), and that it, this simultaneity of high tragedy and dumb comedy, resembles the art of Elvis in "Milkcow" and Murray in *Meatballs* but is most similar to the great works of the Romantic age, such as the *Moby-Dick* of Melville, Byron's *Don Juan*, Keats's great odes. These works share a primary mode of expression: Romantic irony, a subject that I have written about before and that I still find un-put-downably compelling.

Now, there are many different kinds of irony, all grounded on the assumption that something can be both itself and its opposite at the same time. The word comes from the Greek *eiron*, which means "to dissimulate," and was often used to describe a stock character in classical—that is, Greek and Roman—comedy, the tricky guy, usually a wiseass servant who pretends to be helping some big shot get a girl but is in fact working all along to get the girl himself. The audience of the play knows this all along, and this of course creates all sorts of comic situations.

Several kinds of irony grow from this structure. There is dramatic irony, occurring when the audience knows something a character in the play doesn't. Oedipus bellows about how he would bring the source of his city's plague to justice if the perpetrator lived in his very house, which of course he does: the perp is Oedipus himself, whose horrible crimes of incest and patricide, of which he is not aware, are the source of his city's woes. There is also Socratic irony, pretending you don't know anything in order to draw pompous sophists into debate with you so that you can show them that in fact you know a fuckload and they don't know shit. Verbal irony: speaking ironically and apparently knowing you speak ironically, as Jane Austen does at the beginning of *Pride and Prejudice*, where "It is a truth universally acknowledged, that a single man in possession of a good fortune must be in want of a wife" really means the opposite—that is, a single woman in possession of no fortune must be in want of a man who has one. There are other forms, but let's move on, this not being a high school English class.

The type of irony pertinent to Lynch, as well as Melville et al., is, as I said, Romantic, which the Schlegel brothers and their friend Novalis (aka Friedrich von Hardenberg, for whom see Penelope Fitzgerald's breathtaking *The Blue Flower*) developed at the outset of the Romantic period, in 1798. The Romantic ironist believes that the world is too complicated, unpredictable, chaotic, evanescent, mysterious, to ever be accurately described by our words, images, numbers, by any system of human meaning-making. So there exists an ongoing gap between our systems of knowledge and the world these systems are designed to know. And so assertions of knowledge are actually claims of ignorance. This is true for everyone claiming to know anything. What distinguishes the Romantic ironist is that he *realizes* this and finds creative ways to express it.

This sort of ironist might, like Byron in *Don Juan*, write about the process of writing, confessing to the reader, for instance, that he begins his poem hungover, a revelation that calls attention to the fictionality of the verse. Far from a disclosure of reality, the poetry is one possible construction among an infinite number of constructions, a construction especially dubious in this case, since it allegedly originates from a booze haze. Or the romantically ironic writer could, turning to Melville, create a character, like Ishmael, who doesn't tie himself, as crazy Ahab does, to one worldview to the exclusion of all others but attempts rather to experience life from a bewildering number of perspectives, ranging from scientific classification to painting to sculpture to mythology to carving to poetry, more keen on intensity and elasticity than on truth, structure. Or Keats-like, the Romantic ironist might set going a dialogue that will never end, in which the purpose of the conversation is not to reach conclusion but to keep the talk going:

Life: Which is superior, art or life?

Art: Art of course, since it elevates an electric moment above time's flow, crystallizes this riveting instant, illuminates it for all of our meaning-starved gazes.

Life: But isn't that rather static? Without the dynamism of time, there would exist no galvanic glimpses mesmerizing the artist in the first place.

Art: Granted, but to place too much value in temporal fluctuation is to suffer only loss of what one most loves; surely it is better to ponder "the artifices of eternity."

Life: Perhaps. Although that's an old man's time-killing activity, moribund. To be alive: that's to attend to the "sensual music," "salmon-falls," and "mackerel-crowded seas."

Art: Maybe. Sorry I got the Yeats going, when it's Keats's nightingale over which we should be jawboning.

And so on, with each turn in the dialogue, like each wider Emersonian circle, expanding, enriching, enlivening.

In each case—Keats, Melville, Byron—the artist attempts to embody in words the way we actually, if we are honest, experience the world: provisionally, doubting while confirming, improvising as much as planning, composing as does an artist in the midst of his drafting, revising endlessly, keeping what works, casting aside what doesn't, on the lookout for something new to use, or something old to reuse. Self-consciously embracing the process by which we try to understand—as opposed to the final product we might wish our understanding would produce—we become Romantic ironists, affirming and denying at once, asserting, in essence: This conclusion feels true for the present, but I know that it isn't true for all time, and so it's true and not true. Now we dwell in the land of auto-erasure, *Mission: Impossible* realm. This message will self-destruct in five seconds.

And Lynch sends gorgeous missives. He persistently intimates that all representations of the world are indeed understandable and at times noble attempts to translate chaos into order, the void into significance. At the same time, he suggests that these representations are silly gropings to achieve what can't be done: establish legitimate, durable structure and meaning.

44.

But if all serious ideas are ultimately silly (and all ridiculous notions actually somber), then aren't all theories more or less the same, indistinguishable in that they lack ultimate legitimacy, what we like to call truth? As I have been suggesting, no. Some ideas are more powerful than others in that they liberate their beholders into new possibilities for being, possibilities that will enrich their lives and those around them. These are the ideas, often expressed by romantically ironic artists, that actually, in their galvanic intricacy, come closest to the universe's weird superabundance.

This is what the Dadaists, along with the surrealists and situationists, were attempting: to capture in absurd art the universe's absurdity. Woolf's experimental novels, dynamic amalgamations of multitudinous perspectives on ephemeral everydayness, also aspired to express in text the ungraspable fecundity of existence. Dillard's words—paradoxical, duplicitous, ambiguous, dense—gesture toward wordlessness as well, as do of course David Lynch's films, *Inland Empire* in particular, a picture, like Federico Fellini's *8½* or Billy Wilder's *Sun-*

set Boulevard, that depicts how film itself, because of its illusory, tenuous quality (what is it but motion, celluloid, and light?), is the most appropriate medium for capturing the ghostly lubricity of experience. Murray's acting flicks toward this slipperiness as well (so does Grant's), subtly morphing into new personae by the minute, each mask affirming, revising, canceling those that came before, and so capturing the exhilaratingly crazed flux of time itself.

To continue such a list of works that "qualify" as sublime art, highlighting their failure to represent experience in such a way that they succeed, would be ridiculous (although it would be fun, since it would be an excuse to mention William Blake's *The Marriage of Heaven and Hell*, the "Christabel" of Coleridge, Edgar Allan Poe's "Ulalume," Emily Dickinson's "There's a Certain Slant of Light," John Cheever's "Goodbye My Brother" ["I saw them come out and I saw that they were naked, unshy, beautiful, and full of grace, and I watched the naked women walk out of the sea"], Jacques Lacarrière's *The Gnostics*, Malcolm Lowry's *Under the Volcano*, the *Alexandria Quartet* of Lawrence Durrell, *The White Album* of Joan Didion, Penelope Fitzgerald's *The Blue Flower*, Halldór Laxness's *Under the Glacier*, *The Blue Fox* of Sjón, Paul Harding's *Tinkers*, John Berryman's *The Dream Songs* ["These Songs are not meant to be understood, you understand. / They are only meant to terrify & comfort"], John Crowley's *Little, Big*, Bob Dylan and The Band's *Basement Tapes* [especially "Clothes Line Saga," "Yea! Heavy and a Bottle of Bread," "Lo and Behold!," and "Please, Mrs. Henry"], Dylan's "115th Dream," Patti Smith's *Horses* ["Jesus died for somebody's sins but not mine"], William Moore's "Old Country Rock," Jonathan Richman's "Pablo Picasso" ["Pablo Picasso never got called an asshole"], Talking

Heads' "I, Zimbra," "Cities" of same, any square of Mark Rothko, Joan Miró's amoebaesque dots, Edward Gorey's anything, Roman Polanski's *Chinatown*, Jim Jarmusch's *Dead Man*, Sofia Coppola's *Lost in Translation*, Wes Anderson's *Fantastic Mr. Fox*, Nicholas Ray's *In a Lonely Place*, Michael Winterbottom's *The Trip*, Buster Keaton's *Sherlock, Jr.*, and so on).

And it is equally silly to catalog works that lack perpetually playful multiplicity, works straight up, committed to representing a reality that is familiar, reassuring. Either we know what these works are without thinking—predictable genre exercises, clichéd reinforcements of the status quo—or we get into subjective bashing of the so-called artists who stumble into our Academy of the Overrated (first imagined in Woody Allen's *Manhattan*, which by the way should have made the list above, along with *Annie Hall*, but those are terribly obvious choices). But how often do you get an opportunity to say, in print, how uninteresting Billy Collins is, and Lars von Trier (except for *Melancholia*), and The Smiths, and our man the surrealist Salvador Dalí, whose weirdness becomes so predictable as to become more familiar than Grandmother? Well, you get the opportunity all the time if you have a computer and Internet access. So there's nothing special about what I'm doing, except maybe for just now feeling stupid for criticizing these artists, all of whom are probably twenty times the man I am, and sixty times the artist.

Best to turn to the film critic Manny Farber, whose distinction between White Elephant cinema and Termite film captures the contrast I'm making between fakeness whose stylistic failures succeed in gesturing toward the ungraspable actual, and artifices whose structural successes fail to suggest this same inscrutable existence. The latter kind of art is akin to Farber's "[m]asterpiece art, reminiscent of the enameled tobacco humidors and wooden lawn ponies bought at white elephant auctions decades ago." The "[t]hree sins of white elephant art are (1) frame the action with an allover pattern, (2) install every event, character, situation in a frieze of continuities, and (3) treat every inch of the screen and film [or page or canvas] as a potential area for prizeworthy creativity." "Good work," in contrast, "usually arises where the creators seem to have no ambitions towards gilt culture but are involved in a kind of squandering-beaverish endeavor that isn't anywhere or for anything. A peculiar fact about termite–tapeworm–fungus–moss art is that it goes always forward eating its own boundaries, and, likely as not, leaves nothing in its path other than the signs of eager, industrious, unkempt activity."

45.

Forget aesthetic qualities. Some representations of experience, as I have hinted, are more *ethical* than others. So Martha Nochimson, an acquaintance of Lynch's, claims in her most recent book, *David Lynch Swerves*. For her, following Lynch's example, to approximate in art the sublime cosmos discerned by quantum physics is to become morally responsible.

Characters who thrive in Lynch's films are those who embrace quantum weirdness, realizing that certainty, consistency, predictability, logic are reductive fictions in a cosmos teeming with possibilities for connection and creation. Those trying to control the universe—to chop it into self-contained units of matter that they can manipulate into stable, secure systems—envision the world as a "marketplace" (a term Nochimson borrows from Lynch).

Marketplace "refers to the problematic limits of ordinary domestic and public transactions," limits that almost always work in the service of materialism, in the sense of placing too much value on possessing and maintaining stuff that will make one comfortable, content, static, an owner of the American dream. But the marketplace is precisely that: a dream, and a destructive one, limiting one's capacity to grow, love, imagine. The marketplace is indeed a capitalistic nightmare, like the dystopias described by Debord, Baudrillard, and Co.: the cosmos attenuated to meaningless spectacle, though the performers in the play battle to dominate others—by seizing control of the largest amount of stuff, as if the drama were actually real. How to awaken from this nightmare? How to leap into the light of the greenroom, where all the costumes hang and makeup rests, along with a multitude of other scripts, each hinting that we might create billions of characters and plays and forever make the fun flourish?

Lynch thinks that we can find ourselves awake in the wings. Take *Mulholland Dr.*, Lynch's 2001 film, which depicts the Hollywood marketplace and how "people get fatally stuck there," how it can flatten creativity to commodities, commodities that in turn seduce non-Hollywooders, at least geography-wise, to copy them, become merely consumable goods themselves. But the film also explores those moments when Hollywood's "free flows of energy," potential "generators of endless possibilities," break through the imprisoning grids. These moments are rare—like the first sentence of *To the Lighthouse*, an Elvis-spooky *welllll*, a Murrayesque HA!— because we have been so deeply hypnotized by the American dream of "material security and stability" that we fear the "hopeful boundlessness" that is in fact the "genuine source of security." This is Lynch's primary paradox, one lyrically developed, as we know, by Alan Watts: to desire material security is to suffer the endless anxiety of getting, spending, keeping, losing, while to embrace the basic insecurity of matter, quantum matter, bizarrely entangled and superpositioned, is to enjoy lasting stability, a comfort with, and compassion for, what is.

Morally, Lynch's successful characters, his good characters, such as Nikki in *Inland Empire* and Alvin in *The Straight Story*, open to the multiverse, letting, to use Nochimson's words, "creativity happen." They suspend their "stock responses or learned efforts to be certain" and dive into "vital, flowing reality," sensing their oneness with the many, their manifoldness among the unity, and practice compassion toward those with whom they are connected and tolerance toward that from which they are distinct.

Swimming in these crosscurrents, Lynch's noble creations approach Ricoeur's ideal ethical state, which occurs when we expand our awareness of the multiple narrative flows surrounding and pervading our own personal eddies and encompass as many of these currents as possible. Likewise, this Lynchian ethic recalls John Berger, who believed that we should break through the values of the marketplace and strive for "the experience of seeking to give meaning to our lives, of trying to understand the history of which we can become active agents." Hayden White enters this scene as well, thinking that we should be aware of the fictionality of our sense-making narratives and attempt to fabricate stories that are ameliorative rather than oppressive.

When we create life generously and sensitively—you know this—existence is *italicized*, heightened, highlighted, throbbing. The ordinary feels weird; the weird becomes familiar. Anything might happen. Portents and omens are afoot. What storm will break, or geyser rise, or star fall? Our spirits turn as sweet and tender and blue-bright and fragile and sorrowful as autumn. The readiness, Hamlet, is all.

46.

When you're not ready enough, old-fashioned realism reigns. You assume that what you see is what you get and believe that the artist, yourself, and everyone else should mimic the given. But when you're *too* ready, irony simply for the sake of irony dominates, endless reflection upon reflection upon reflection, no end in sight, and artists—ourselves—merely enter into states of "n + 1–ness," exhausting themselves into po-mo-nihilistico apathy. If you can doubt everything, why bother doing anything?

Our most famous and accomplished realist is Jonathan Franzen, composing his Dickens-like tomes—*The Corrections*, *Freedom*—on recognizable, "everyday" characters negotiating current cultural forces. He favors the third-person omniscient narrator, the eye in the sky, objectively recording earthlings' goings-on. And our most well-known and brilliant postmodernist would be David Foster Wallace himself, whose thousand-page *Infinite Jest* combines a multitude of styles, voices, and genres, many of which receive highly self-aware commentary in a lengthy section of footnotes. You walk away from Franzen thinking, "There's a world and it's serious," while you stagger from Wallace, spinning dizzily in the thought "There are only words, words, words, around the void whirling, and nothing to do, if you even want to sniff something resembling reality, but show that you know this."

Wallace, though, was troubled by the postmodern techniques he so stunningly practiced, believing that they could result only in hollow metafiction, or fiction about fiction: I am writing a fiction; I am aware that I am writing a fiction; I am aware that I am aware that I am writing a fiction; and so on. Wallace wanted to transcend this kind of writing, ultimately narcissistic in its obsessive self-regard—like Hamlet overly ready, *way*, basically on cognitive crack—and likely to lead, as too much reflecting did for the Black Prince (and the bandannaed Wallace), to paralyzing, suicide-inducing depression.

Wallace couldn't return to conventional realism, though, suspecting it to be the most banal and uninteresting of shams. So, he wondered, what kind of sincerity could be ironic and earnest at the same time? He described the shape such authenticity might take in his famous Kenyon College commencement address, from 2005, titled "This Is Water": to be truly educated, he claims, "means being conscious and aware enough to choose what you pay attention to and to choose how you construct meaning from experience."

> If you're aware enough to give yourself a choice, you can choose to look differently at this fat, dead-eyed, over-made-up lady who just screamed at her kid in the checkout line. Maybe she's not usually like this. Maybe she's been up three straight nights holding the hand of a husband who is dying of bone cancer. Or maybe this very lady is the

low-wage clerk at the motor vehicle department, who just yesterday helped your spouse resolve a horrific, infuriating, red-tape problem through some small act of bureaucratic kindness. Of course, none of this is likely, but it's also not impossible. It just depends what you want to consider. If you're automatically sure that you know what reality is, and you are operating on your default setting, then you, like me, probably won't consider possibilities that aren't annoying and miserable. But if you really learn how to pay attention, then you will know there are other options. It will actually be within your power to experience a crowded, hot, slow, consumer-hell type situation as not only meaningful, but sacred, on fire with the same force that made the stars: love, fellowship, the mystical oneness of all things deep down.

Then the ever-reflective, and humble and self-effacing Wallace admits, "not that that mystical stuff is necessarily true." But what is true, "capital-T True," is "that you get to decide how you're gonna try to see it."

Call this aesthetic pragmatism. Call it Romantic irony. Call it the new sincerity (apparently a movement). Or perhaps term it, after reading a fine scholarly article by Timotheus Vermeulen and Robin van den Akker, metamodernism. It, whatever this *is*, results in transforming the woman in the checkout from boringly annoying to resplendent saint (or the game of cricket, played by the ocean, into redemption, or the stark winter light into a revelation of melancholy's meaning). In each case the artist—and we all are artists, good, bad, or ugly—expands the ordinary into the extraordinary or condenses the extraordinary into the common. He, she, enchants the cosmos.

Real magic: believing is seeing; seeing, acting. Wallace

imaginatively transubstantiates the checkout woman into a paragon of compassion wearied into consternation. Is that enough? It is something, sublime, a reorientation that turns annoyance or resignation or boredom into almost mystical community. But more, the sweet, inexhaustible *more*, would be: Wallace *says* to the harried woman, a *kind* thing—even if it's a cliché, a lie, like chuckling bright-facedly, "Those kids of yours are sure spirited," or, in a soft voice, saying, "Looks like you've got your hands full." These lines might relieve the woman's burden for just a second, recall her to better moments. Who knows? Such lines, though, could just as easily make the situation worse, might irritate the woman more, coming across as intrusive or just as annoying as the little ones.

This sounds like stupid stuff, the mundane made moral. It probably is, but sometimes these little niceties, for all their shallowness, can make all the difference. Like the day I went into a New York deli, hungover, depressed, lonely, hungry, nonlabyrinthine as Jedediah Purdy (who I bet is a light drinker), having little money in my pocket, and the guy making my sandwich—turkey and provolone on white—said to me, so gently, as he was finishing up, "You wanna a little bacon?" and when I said no, knowing the extra cost for this, he continued, "Okay, but I got it here, might as well throw it on there, no charge," and I nodded okay, and then he laid those perfectly fried strips on the sandwich as if they were sacred wafers, and as he completed the meal and wrapped it snugly in paper and then handed it to me, smiling, I really did feel better—less alone, more hopeful—since in this cruel universe a person can be merciful, giving a stranger a boon whether the stranger deserves it or not—deserving in fact being beyond, entirely, the question—for that's what mercy, earth's greatest fiction, is:

treating someone "as if" he were worthy, and rewarding him, when in fact that person, like all of us, is inwardly criminal or on the outside. Who should 'scape whipping, Grim Dane?

God's bodykins, this *is* stupid stuff. Yes. We would—I would—feel more hopeful if Wallace's metamorphosing imagination had generated not just his own inner calm or a kind passing word for a tired woman managing two howling brats but also a more lasting change: Wallace, sensitive to suffering and aware of his special power to ameliorate it, becoming more affectionate and understanding to those he loves or offering to volunteer (as Wallace, bless him, did) to help others, the homeless, the impoverished, maybe stray cats and dogs. (Apparently Wallace at one point, when his writing was coming hard, thought he might run an animal shelter for a living.) And surely such profound, lovely transformations occur all the time, short-term or long, and are certainly more substantial by far than the ten-second faux social chitchat at the checkout, however kindly intended.

Mock me for being sentimental, with my little Dickensian tales of charity's unexpected birth and prospering. But, as Wallace says, sometimes those clichés by which we attenuate existence's depths into tepid dishwater can, if we take them seriously for just a second—*bad taste* to go on too long—bloom from the banal into the beautiful: *take it one day at a time*; *the longest journey begins with a single step*; *be here now*; *fake it till you make it*. To imagine these flattenings of life's complexities as pragmatic directions expands them into intricate maps to the heroic: character, fortitude, creativity, flexibility, grace.

47.

Depression whipped me into grace. (I have published versions of this story before too, but not in this context, or toward this end.) Just as terminal cancer might make a man love his wife or his rosebush with more intensity than before, or as winter generates passion for spring, so my depression taught me what I needed to keep from committing suicide, which, believe me, I thought about, with more precision and frequency than I did the grocery list or the plans to build my daughter's sleeping loft or writing this book, thought about every hour during every day. In the midmorning department meeting, before the postlunch chair nap, during my run later on, and at night, I had visions in my head, Blu-ray lucid, of going into the basement, where my father's old shotgun leaned behind the boiler, and exploding my skull, chunks of my brain splattering the 1915 brick; or of throwing myself down my house's stairs one still-dark morning, my neck breaking about halfway, and there I am dead at the bottom; or of emptying a bottle of Ambien into the back of my throat and then swallowing the pills down with half a bottle of Bombay gin, just like in the movies; or of hanging myself; or of asphyxiating on exhaust; or of driving off a cliff; or of leaping in front of a car or a train. Really everything but drowning, in that regard, lacking the courage of Woolf, who weighted her pockets with stones and walked into the river Ouse.

In junior high, I often slipped into my room after dinner and lay a long time in the darkness, thinking weird and morbid thoughts, relieved to be free of the judging gaze of my parents, teachers, anyone, really, in town; in high school, I often couldn't sleep the whole night, nervous about nothing, and sometimes decided that I wouldn't say a word to anyone at school for days; after leaving West Point, I became a triathlete, trained three to four hours a day, starved myself, slept three hours a night, went into serious funks when I got any grade below an A; once I reached grad school, I stayed in bed entire weekends, the lights low, refused to answer the door or return phone calls, and started drinking a six-pack of cheap lager every night. I assumed that all these activities were normal for someone self-conscious, ambitious, thoughtful, cynical, morbid.

But in the days following the birth of my first and only child, sweet Una, the brooding turned suicidal, and the anxiety became mania. During the years before her birth, I exhausted these increasingly intense negative feelings by working, working, twelve, fourteen hours a day: reading, researching, writing, teaching, grading, motivating myself by the promise of praise, success, accolades. I also drank heavily, martini after martini, once the day's labors were done. But when Una was born, these habits were compromised. By choice. I could have continued them, neglected child and wife, but I wanted to be a good father and an improved husband.

So I found myself at the age of thirty-five, forced to face what my working and drinking, now diminished, helped me hide: I was a deeply sad, anxious man, vacillating between the pain over my failure to make anything feel meaningful and my numbness toward the failure. The hurt pushed me toward suicide. The apathy might as well have killed me. Both exhausted me, as did my constant performing of the roles of father and husband, rote, mechanical, soulless.

How I groped from this deadening mixture of indifference and despair to a psychiatrist remains a mystery. Maybe it was the fear that if I didn't come back to life, my wife would leave me, taking my child, who would soon not know or care about me, who would have another man for a father. Maybe it was some internal will to live, evolutionary or spiritual, that overpowered my death drive. Luck, possibly.

I found a psychiatrist who gave me my current bipolar diagnosis and prescribed medicines that actually helped, lowering the suicide sirens to a background hum and so giving me barely enough tranquillity to imagine a life beyond the cemetery.

This psychiatrist also recommended that I see a psychotherapist for weekly counseling. This man emphasized that I am not simply equal to my biochemistry, which is killing me, but greater than, able to alter how I see the world and act within it. How to express this power? Through implementing a therapeutic pragmatism close to that of William James (though this psychotherapist—let's call him Dr. S.—had never, to my knowledge, read James).

Dr. S. probably learned a version of James's pragmatism from the Landmark Forum, which I attended, at his behest, one long weekend, painful—since I held to my vow not to drink alcohol during that time. I had to sit for about thirty-seven hours a day in a dingy chain hotel conference room and confront all my hidden hang-ups, fears, misplaced commitments, sometimes verbally, in front of total strangers—but powerful, too, this weekend, because of the primary idea: outside of our meaning-making narratives, nothing is. So if your life is not going well, *change* your narrative.

According to Dr. S., I was currently the author of a novel in which I, as the protagonist, was a loser. That's what he said, and he meant it. He argued that in my narrative, I had it that—he loved that phrase, "had it that"—the depression was controlling me, and I need not be responsible for my actions. "How can I be expected to be a good husband or father," I was tacitly whispering to myself (according to Dr. S.), "while I'm suffering from bipolar disorder, which is all the time? You wouldn't expect a cancer patient to run a marathon, would you? No. Then why would you expect me, ripped between mania and depression, to be open, affectionate, intimate, energetic?"

Having it this way, I was, Dr. S. opined, addicting myself to victimhood, one of the perverse pleasures of the weak. Even though the victim is oppressed, mistreated, imprisoned, he often savors his role, because he is free of responsibility. He can do whatever he wants and blame it on the oppressor. To have it this way, however, is to alienate oneself from fertile human relationships, which require agency (choosing one action over another) and responsibility (following through on what one vows to do).

Dr. S. maintained—no, bellowed, for he was a *crazy man*, not afraid to go to the floor and scream to make a point—that I would never be able to be a good father or husband, or indeed person in general, and never be able to find a jot of joy until I stopped treating my depression as a tyrant determining all my moves. I needed a new narrative.

"Go home, Eric," Dr. S. urged. "You're an English major guy and so should enjoy this; construct a new book of life, a novel in which you as protagonist have power and grace."

And damned if I did, more out of arrogance, I suspect, than desire to get better; being a victim, let me tell you, is weirdly enjoyable, in a totally destructive sort of way. I wanted to show Dr. S. that I was creative, able to fashion a work more beautiful than any he'd ever encountered.

I established the principles behind my new novel. First, my depression is simply a part of me, not the cruel controller, no different in kind from my lungs, foot, or heart, so, I can shape it, just as I do my breathing, beating, leaping. Second, my depression, though painful, is also a gift, since it has fostered a contemplative life, my propensities to brood over the meaning of suffering, loneliness, despair. It has also revealed to me what I need to feel intensely alive, surrounding me with a darkness that can be broken only by the strongest beam.

With these ideas as my starting points, I reimagined my life, viewing my periods of greatest depression as natural parts of my development, times, indeed, of greatest spiritual growth.

That was as far as I got before seeing Dr. S. again, a kind of outline or proposal. When I told him about it, he stared at me for about fifteen seconds before screaming, "You get an F, Professor!"

I said, "Hey man, you just fucking with me?"

"No. I gave you a failing grade because your little proposal isn't about you wanting to connect more intimately with your family; it's about you trying to show off for me. I can see right through your bullshit. Go back and start over, this time with more specific actions. In fact, that's your homework: come up with one new habit and carry it out once a day. Don't worry about writing the narrative; it's too tempting for you to try to be clever, which you've been your whole life, as a way of defending yourself against real intimacy, which requires vulnerability. If you make everything a joke, then nothing's serious. C'mon, man. Get serious for once."

So I went home and tried to ignore Dr. S.'s F, convincing myself that he had failed me just to keep me on my toes, in the same way that I sometimes, as a professor, return papers ungraded, saying they're not even good enough at this point to get an H.

But I couldn't. He was right. I was more interested in appearing intelligent than in getting better. I reconsidered the new assignment: just create a new habit. Less grandiose than novel writing but also more *doable*. But what to do?

It came to me. I will forget being a PARENT, all responsible and serious, and become *Crazy Dad*, like a sitcom character, my sole goal being to make Una laugh, laugh, laugh. I know. Sounds stupid. But it's what I thought, probably because this habit allowed me to do what I was best at, performing.

I as Crazy Dad made a strange game for me and Una, at the time four, to play. I was a teacher, and my class was composed of Una, several stuffed animals, some blocks, and a ficus tree. I called roll as though it were the first day of class, giving each student, with Una's help, a ridiculous name. Una answered for each creature, "Here." As I neared the end of the roll, I fell into an epileptic fit, flinging a book or two—gently—around the room, mimicking a professor having a nervous breakdown in front of class. Una would laugh epileptically herself, and we had a fine old time, better than we had ever had, and grew closer each time we played, more at ease with each other, and I actually starting desiring to be with her, not out of duty but pleasure.

I won't bore you with the other such absurd games she and I created, though one involved attempting to capture the voice of a toad in a foul mood that speaks only French and is lost in Russia, in terrible need of food. Recounting parent-child games is almost as bad as telling a group of the dream you had last night: after the first sentence, all auditors brace and endure.

To say that Dada saved Dad is sort of true here, since the happy consequences of my newly created Crazy Dad role inspired me to fashion other roles, not as crazy and not just to foster more satisfying relationships with my daughter—with my wife, too, and my friends. And the performances—some much more successful than others—helped ease the depression's pain.

They kept me aware of the cognitive distance between my bipolar biochemistry (my brain) and my interpretive capacities (my mind). Calling myself Crazy Dad, instead of Depressed Parent, and acting as though this identity were real and so enjoying a more zany, capricious, playful, capacious, love-charged, creative existence: these behaviors illustrated to me repeatedly the power of my imagination.

Performing thus, I resembled a madcap Chaplin pushed from a tightrope into a lake. Gravity, like biochemistry, controlled my tramp ass, limited my choices. I couldn't Wile E. Coyote–like climb back up to the edge on air (only to fall again, waving a resigned bye-bye on the way down), just as I couldn't will happy neurons. But I could choose *how to fall.* I could flail and scream and belly-slap the water and gasp and sputter and, once under, come close to drowning, thinking, "I'm gonna die!" Or I could relax into the downward rush, execute a flip or a gainer (a little un*gain*ly, though—this *is* slapstick) before cutting into the ripples like a knife, splashlessly, in charge of breath and body, dipping into the depths about ten feet before arching upward and shooting through the brown-green-blue shimmery water with the shabby, soggy grace of Charlie himself.

Gravity, marker of what we can't do, becomes, for the slapstick performer, a muse to what he can. He is able to transform the downward push into leaps ten laughs high. And so, when I was successfully performing a happy role, my depression morphed from sign of my limitation to enabler of my imagination. Performing, reminding myself of my ability endlessly to perform and of the transformative powers of the acting, I experienced what those depressed lack: *hope.*

Dante was right. Hell is the abandonment of hope, existing with no future toward which to raise the anticipatory gaze, enjoying no vibrant past out of which this exciting future will grow, but rather stuck in a dismal present, static as a stake stabbed. Purgatory and paradise, though, are imbued with hope, that sweet sense that life develops, dramatically expanding and contracting, decaying and recovering, pushing toward a grand purpose.

I am far from cured; never will be. I'm not a positive person. I still go stupid with gloom and get fevered with mania. But now I know I am not a victim of my disorder, and so, when the depression wrestles me down, I fight back, for days, weeks, however long it takes, and subdue the creature once more. It will slap me down again another day, and another day I will give as good as I get, and this will be the drama of my life, perpetual conflict and resolution, eminently worth undergoing, because from this play I can learn how to love even though I lose and grow more generous in spite of my pettiness.

48.

Even if it's all fake, profound distinctions exist: between evil and good, lie and truth, engineered and grown, destructive and healthy, Frey and Dillard. The distinctions can be drawn according to the pragmatic rule: the more salubrious for the greater number of creatures, the truer; the more destructive, increasing falseness.

Imagine a continuum: on one side, A, all beings thriving in an immense ecosystem, marvelously symbiotic, gorgeous; on the other side, Z, a war-scorched waste, all things at constant odds, each either dominating or in terrified flight.

Occurrences press one direction or the other, with most falling somewhere close to the middle.

Close to Z: lying in order to gain power over another; altering food DNA in the name of greed, thus compromising wide environments; interfacing with the virtual world until the mind behaves like a computer. Farther away, but still with a Z-ward tilt: trying to pass fictions as fact in the name of fame; undergoing cosmetic surgery to conform to Madison

Avenue fantasies; believing the politician's performed authenticity is really real.

Nearing Alphaville: create words that inspire others to do the same; farm organically; converse face-to-face, in an unwired room. Sliding slightly toward the middle, but still in sight of A: exaggerate your best cat story in the name of good poetry, lift weights to look like Christian Bale in *Batman*, or throw potato salad at a pompous professor of Dada.

Where does Wilson fall on this line? Where do you? All over the fucking place, in my case and most likely in yours. But I know where A is, remember how to push toward it.

49.

Here is a map. Late in life, St. Francis was going blind. The pope ordered him to have his eyes operated on so he could retain his vision. The primitive operation required that his face be cauterized. As the fiery iron neared his skin, Francis said: "Brother Fire, God made you beautiful and strong and useful. I pray that you be courteous to me." Of this scene, G. K. Chesterton said: "If life is art, this is a masterpiece moment."

50.

In 1988 Errol Morris released *The Thin Blue Line*, a documentary in which he examined the case of the convicted murderer Randall Adams. Morris was so tenacious for the truth that he proved what the courts had missed, Adams's innocence. A year after the movie came out, Adams was freed and so avoided a life sentence, thirteen years of which he had already served.

Morris's doggedness for what really happened has inspired two other films, *The Fog of War* and *The Unknown Known*, both of which uncover the lies that powerful statesmen—Robert McNamara and Donald Rumsfeld, respectively—deployed to justify wars. Not surprisingly, Morris worked as a private investigator before becoming a documentarian.

Morris's passion for the facts was aired recently on an episode of the NPR show *Radiolab*. The piece focused on Morris's quest to discover the sequence of two pictures taken by Roger Fenton, one of the first photographers to document war, the Crimean War in this case. In 1855 Fenton took a picture of a desolate valley in the war zone, through which runs, into the gray horizon, a lonely dirt road. It is strewn with cannonballs. Fenton called it *The Valley of the Shadow of Death*. But another version of the same scene, apparently taken the same day, is also extant. Everything is apparently the same, save one detail: the cannonballs lie to the left of the road, in a ditch.

These two versions have led several experts to conclude that one of the earliest war photographs was also one of the first staged photographs, the assumption being that Fenton found his first composition, the "real" one, cannonballs off road, to be lacking and so rearranged the details to his liking: balls on road.

Morris didn't so much question the fake-photo hypothesis as the assumption that the off-road occurred before the on-road. He admitted that one could certainly reasonably assume that the on-road was second, since it is more "aesthetic," ostensibly illustrating that "the way is blocked with the horrors of war." But Morris also claimed that one could with just as much validity assume that the off-road was second, because it suggests its own stagedness. In the midst of war's hell, hope remains: a way cleared of obstacles.

Hungry to know which came first, Morris interviewed art historians. He also visited the actual site where the photos were shot. He found nothing. Then he ran into a friend, Dennis Purcell, at a party. He thought Purcell, an optical engineer, might be of help. After much study, Purcell revealed that three pebbles were lower down the bank in the on-road image. He concluded that Fenton and his helpers inadvertently kicked the stones down the bank when transporting the balls from ditch to road. Off-road indeed came first: what really happened minus the artist's intervention. Then Fenton meddled, transmogrified the spheres into a parable.

For Morris, problem solved: the first photo is *authentic*. But Purcell, the forensic catalyst of Errol's satisfaction, feels otherwise. He believes that the second, on-road, is more valid, because it expresses the "emotional truth" of the scene. A true artist, Fenton altered the cannonballs "to make [the landscape] look the way it felt."

To which Morris says, "Forget all that." What he ultimately took from his search for the Crimean sequence, he confessed on *Radiolab*, was not which image was more authentic but the way the relationship between the photographs made him *feel* the motion of the stones and inspired intense empathy with the soldiers, with their "feet hitting the rocks," their "walking" through that desolation, the complex physical "reality of the scene." In slipping through the gap between these photos, as if "through a pinhole camera," Morris recalled his father, who had died when Morris was two. He only knew his dad through black-and-white photographs. Now, scrutinizing the shadowy images of his parent as he had earlier studied Fenton's cannonballs, he asked with renewed force, "Who was this man? What is the mystery of this man?" He couldn't answer. He could only march once more through his own desolate valley, where all that we most love is lost.

But in bearing witness to the shadows of what has passed—the memorial pictures, the eulogizing words—we can find a kind of grace, the resurrection, within our hearts, of the one gone, more alive to us now than when we could actually touch his hand, because we understand how abundant he was, how able to fill the emptiness now within us, and we imagine that fecundity and are nourished. The thirsty man learns the water, Emily Dickinson writes, so much more acutely than the quenched, just as Plato's men, cave shackled and blinded, understand most resplendently the glaring air.

This book has been about how we fake it to compensate for what we lack, to make up for the ruining of love in the books of our days. Build your own artifice out of the rubble, maybe a sphere expansive as the universe, or perhaps a single ball, apple size. How well it fits into your hand. You throw it across the field easily, and your daughter catches it every time.

BIBLIOGRAPHICAL NOTES

1.

A detailed study of the first words of babies is Twila Tardif, Paul Fletcher, Weilan Liang, Zhixiang Zhang, Nico Kaciroti, and Virginia A. Marchman, "Baby's First 10 Words," *Developmental Psychology* 44.4 (2008), pp. 929–38. Laurence Sterne in *The Life and Opinions of Tristram Shandy, Gentleman* (1759–1767) is so acutely aware on the nonlinearity of a personal narrative that he sometimes forgoes language to describe his protagonist's life and resorts to squiggly lines on an otherwise blank page. That language shapes thought and perception is not a new theory. It goes back to the 1930s, when Edward Sapir and Benjamin Lee Whorf concluded, after studying a variety of cultures, that different lexicons produce different experiences. Only recently has the Sapir-Whorf hypothesis been substantiated by empirical data. For a discussion of recent developments of the theory, see Lera Boroditsky, "How Language Shapes Thought: The Languages We Speak Affect Our Perceptions of the World," *Scientific American* (February 2011), pp. 63–65.

2.

Astaire danced this famous sequence in blackface, as a tribute to Bill Robinson, otherwise known as Bojangles. The choice remains controversial, with some viewing it as racist and others as a suitable tribute to a master. For a discussion of both sides of the argument, see Alistair

Macaulay's "Astaire the Artist, Even in Blackface," *New York Times*, January 27, 2011, p. AR 5. The scholar M. H. Abrams followed Romantic poets like Blake, Wordsworth, and Shelley in envisioning the mind as mirror and lamp, finding reality and creating it at once, in his seminal study *The Mirror and the Lamp: Romantic Theory and the Critical Tradition* (New York: Oxford University Press, 1971). William Blake said in a letter to one Reverend Dr. John Trusler, "As a man is So he Sees."

3.

In Forster's *Howards End* (1910), Margaret Schlegel (played beautifully by Emma Thompson in the 1992 Merchant-Ivory film production of the novel) thinks, "Only connect! That was the whole of her sermon. Only connect the prose and the passion, and both will be exalted, and human love will be seen at its height. Live in fragments no longer. Only connect, and the beast and the monk, robbed of the isolation that is life to either, will die." D. H. Lawrence's poem "Bavarian Gentians" (1932) describes the flowers as "darkening the daytime torchlike with the smoking blueness of Pluto's gloom." Lawrence also wrote a book, in prose, titled *Etruscan Places* (1932), in which he praises Etruscan culture for its celebration of elegant transience over pompous stonework, a paean that prompts him to ask: "Why has mankind had such a craving to be imposed upon? Why this lust after imposing creeds, imposing deeds, imposing buildings, imposing language, imposing works of art? The thing becomes an imposition and a weariness at last. Give us things that are alive and flexible, which won't last too long and become an obstruction and a weariness. Even Michelangelo becomes at last a lump and a burden and a bore. It is so hard to see past him" (*Etruscan Places: Travels Through Forgotten Italy* [London: Tauris Parke, 2011], p. 52). This passage and others like it in Lawrence's Etruscan essays inspired me to visit a famous vie cave—a road carved through tufa rock—near Pitigliano. The road is narrow, maybe five feet wide, and cobblestoned. The rock walls on either side tower to fifteen feet or more—or so I remember—and often curve slightly inward at their pinnacles. The effect is like walking through a deep cave whose roof has vanished. Strange words are carved into the tufa, but they aren't as spooky as the death hovels dug into the walls. One twilight ten years ago, my wife, Sandi, and I walked into the corridor. No one else was there. If I had vanished from this world and appeared in another I had barely dreamed or read about, I would have been more thankful than scared. As for fake celebrity Twitter accounts—the fake God now has about 1.4 million followers, and the phony Poe has around 100,000.

4.

I would probably never have listened to Elvis's bodacious milkcow song or Dock Boggs's "Country Blues" if it hadn't been for Greil Marcus, whose 1975 *Mystery Train* (New York: Plume, 2008) and 1997 *Invisible Republic* (New York: Henry Holt, 1997) opened me to the lyrical weirdness of the music of the American Southeast. The bee-sipping poison routine comes from Keats's "Ode on Melancholy" (1819), the first longish poem I ever memorized. Once I was giving an after-dinner speech to university luminaries on my 2008 book *Against Happiness.* By the time I walked hesitantly to the podium, I realized that the open bar had done its duty. I was three minutes into my talk on the wisdom of melancholy when I forgot what the fuck I had planned to say. I kept my wits, though, and solemnly announced, "But who am I to extol the virtues of sorrow? The poet, I believe, said it best," and then I recited, in full, the poem, followed by a humble bow to the audience and a stepping to the side. The applause was thunderous, and I soon found that men and women both had gotten teary. I tell my students: Always keep a memorized poem in your back pocket. I learned about Shelley's swimming, or lack thereof, as well as his passion for water in general, in Ann Wroe's *Being Shelley: The Poet's Search for Himself* (New York: Pantheon, 2007), pp. 109–37. As my mom used to tell me, for shock value, the fitness guru Jack LaLanne used to drink a glass of cow's blood every day back when he was in his thirties. (That would be in the 1940s.) You can find a riveting account of Emerson's visit to Ellen's tomb in Robert D. Richardson, Jr.'s *Emerson: The Mind on Fire* (Berkeley: University of California Press, 1996). The account occurs in the first pages. According to Richardson during a visit to one of my classes at Wake Forest (he is a wonderful, generous man, as well as a brilliant one), his wife, Annie Dillard, had suggested that he move this shocking moment to the beginning of his biography. It was the event in Emerson's life that disturbed him most. In facing this occurrence from the beginning of his book, Richardson was following the advice that Mary Moody Emerson gave to Emerson, her nephew: "Do what you are afraid to do." I repeat this to my creative writing students all the time. In a July 3, 2001, *New York Times* article on the actor Justin Theroux, John Leland noted Theroux's eclectic hipster gothic decorating style, which included a "collection of mousetraps by the bookshelves, a small pile of switchblades on the coffee table and a human skull, a remnant of looser times on eBay, by the side of the couch." I love Theroux for his work in the great Lynch film *Mulholland Dr.*, from 2001, but this article makes him seem as if he was trying too hard to be cool—he was rolling cigarettes and sporting "blackburns and an unstinted [nice phrase, John Leland] pomade." Still, I thought it would be boss to have a skull.

5.

The famous allegory of the cave appears in Book VII of *The Republic* (c. 380 B.C.). It is spoken by Plato's fictional version of his philosophical mentor, Socrates. Cicero tells the story of bees gathering on the baby Plato's tongue in his *Concerning Divination*, Book 1 (44 B.C.).

6.

Pollan discusses the potato beetle in *The Botany of Desire* (New York: Random House, 2001), pp. 186–226, as well as in his seminal article "Playing God in the Garden," *New York Times Magazine*, October 25, 1998. I learned from the website of the U.S. Department of Agriculture's Economic Research Service that upward of 170 million acres are now planted with genetically engineered seeds. See Jorge Fernandez-Cornejo, Seth James Wechsler, and Michael Livingston, "Adoption of Genetically Engineered Crops by U.S. Farmers Has Increased Steadily for over 15 Years," March 4, 2014, www.ers.usda.gov/amber-waves/2014 -march/adoption-of-genetically-engineered-crops-by-us-farmers-has -increased-steadily-for-over-15-years.aspx#.U7GSMEDUEno. Pollan has published two other books on the joys of organic food and the ills of scientifically produced food: *The Omnivore's Dilemma: A Natural History of Four Meals* (New York: Penguin, 2006) and *In Defense of Food: An Eater's Manifesto* (New York: Penguin, 2008). Carr tells the story of Nietzsche in *The Shallows* (New York: Norton, 2010), pp. 17–19. The quotation from

Nietzsche's composer friend comes from p. 19. Other recent books on the ills of our newest technologies are Sherry Turkle's *Alone Together: Why We Expect More from Technology and Less from Each Other* (New York: Basic Books, 2011), Mark Bauerlein's *The Digital Divide: Arguments For and Against Facebook, Google, Texting, and the Age of Social Networking* (New York: Tarcher, 2011), Bauerlein's *The Dumbest Generation: How the Digital Age Stupefies Young Americans and Jeopardizes Our Future (or, Don't Trust Anyone Under 30)* (New York: Tarcher, 2008), Jaron Lanier's *You Are Not a Gadget: A Manifesto* (New York: Knopf, 2010), and Susan Greenfield's *Tomorrow's People: How 21st-Century Technology Is Changing the Way We Think and Feel* (New York: Penguin, 2009).

7.

When I studied for exams in college, I would glob a drop of Elmer's on my right index finger, let it dry for five minutes, and then rub it between finger and thumb until I made a little glue ball, which I would flick into the trash can, and start again. The desk where I sat came with the apartment, and the glue just happened to be in the drawer, left behind by another student. Whenever I whiff the odor of Elmer's (and having a young child I do often), I have Proustian recollections, pleasant, of learning the opening lines of *The Canterbury Tales* in Middle English.

8.

The quote from Vonnegut appears on the frontispiece of *Cat's Cradle*, from 1963. A good friend of mine once offered a great example of foma in practice. For some odd reason you touch the underside of a table in the library. Your index finger feels what might be a dried booger. You say, "Oh, it's just glue," and proceed, un-grossed-out. Salinger's quote appears in *The Catcher in the Rye* (New York: Little, Brown, 1991), p. 22. The novel was first published in 1951. Eliot's lines appear in "Burnt Norton," first published in 1936 and then published as one of the *Four Quartets* in 1944. It is Poe's unnamed narrator in "Ligeia" who may or may not have, while high on opium, poisoned his wife, Rowena, hating her because she wasn't his first wife, Ligeia, who had died. The Wikipedia entry "Lie" can be found at www.en.wikipedia.org/wiki/Lie.

9.

Even if "lying" as a valid concept is strangely reassuring on a metaphysical level, establishing as it does the distinction between what is and isn't, intentional fakery, if left unchecked, can, as the philosopher Sissela Bok argues in her book *Lying*, spread through a society like a virus, spawning imitations or retaliations or forestallings of "suspected deception," and so damages trust, a "social good to be protected just as much as the air we breathe or the water we drink. When it is damaged, the community as a whole suffers; and when it is destroyed, societies falter and collapse" (*Lying: Moral Choice in Public and Private Life* [New York: Vintage, 1999], p. 26). The quotation from *Invisible Republic: Bob Dylan's Basement Tapes* (New York: Henry Holt, 1997) is on p. 67. The book was later rereleased under the title *The Old, Weird America.* The quotation from *Lipstick Traces: A Secret History of the Twentieth Century* (Cambridge, MA: Harvard University Press, 1989) appears on p. 3. For an excellent introduction to how "common sense" is an ideological construct, see Catherine Belsey's *Critical Practice*, 2nd ed. (New York: Routledge, 2002), especially pp. 1–40. I have drawn from these pages in this section. The quotation from Dyer's *Out of Sheer Rage: Wrestling with D. H. Lawrence* (New York: Picador, 2009) is on p. 152. The quotation on "mystification" from Berger's *Ways of Seeing: Based on the BBC Television Series* (New York: Penguin, 1990) can be found on p. 11. Berger's discussion of the painter Frans Hals appears on pp. 12–14. His lines on seeing through the "eyes of a pauper" are on p. 15. The passage on agency appears on p. 33.

10.

I draw my discussion of the relationships between home, work, and leisure from Henri Lefebvre's *Critique of Everyday Life*, vol. 1, trans. John Moore, pref. Michel Trebitsch (London: Verso, 1991); Guy Debord's *The Society of the Spectacle*, trans. Donald Nicholson-Smith (New York: Zone, 1995); and Greil Marcus's *Lipstick Traces* (Cambridge, Mass.: Harvard University Press, 1990), each of which demonstrates how modern capitalism organizes every part of our everyday lives. The quote from Debord on "spectacle" appears on p. 12 of *The Society of the Spectacle.* The passage on "being into having" and "having into *appearing*" is from

p. 16. The lines on celebrity and dissatisfaction appear on p. 38. I first learned about Debord by reading Marcus's *Lipstick Traces.*

12.

This work by Borges can be found in his *Collected Fictions,* trans. Andrew Hurley (New York: Penguin, 1999). A wonderful discussion of it appears in John Irwin's *The Mystery to a Solution: Poe, Borges, and the Analytic Detective Story* (Baltimore: Johns Hopkins University Press, 1966). The quotations by Baudrillard open his *Simulacra and Simulation,* trans. Sheila Faria Glaser (Ann Arbor: University of Michigan Press, 1995).

13.

In *The Decline of the West* (1918–1922), Oswald Spengler shows how modern Western culture is "Faustian" in its desire for technological mastery. An excellent discussion of how we have removed "clinicized" death can be found in Gary Laderman's *Rest in Peace: A Cultural History of Death and the Funeral Home in Twentieth-Century America* (New York: Oxford University Press, 2005).

14.

White's *Metahistory: The Historical Imagination in Nineteenth-Century Europe* (Baltimore: Johns Hopkins University Press, 1975) describes, wittingly or no, the methodology practiced by Paul Fussell in his great 1970 volume *The Great War and Modern Memory,* which explores the narratives World War I soldiers constructed to make sense of their horrors. The quotation from White comes from his essay "The Historical Text as Literary Artifact," collected in *The History and Narrative Reader,* ed. Geoffrey Roberts (New York: Routledge, 2001), p. 235. Kuhn is clear: his is not a "relativist's position," and he does believe in "scientific progress" (*The Structure of Scientific Revolutions,* intro. Ian Hacking, 4th ed [Chicago: University of Chicago Press, 2012], p. 205). If one were to take the successive paradigms of Western science and jumble them up, Kuhn believes, we could return them to their original order by discovering true progress: modern science improves on medieval, say, because modern explains what we experience in more plausible detail. Emerson alludes to this story of Galileo in his essay "Experience," from 1844, when he celebrates the fact that transience saves us from constant despair: "The secret of the illusoriness is in the necessity of a succession of moods or objects. Gladly we would anchor, but the anchorage is quicksand. This onward trick of nature is too strong for us: *Pero* [*sic*] *si muove*. When, at night, I look at the moon and stars, I seem stationary, and they to hurry. Our love of the real draws us to permanence, but health of body consists in circulation, and sanity of mind in variety or facility of association. We need change of objects. Dedication to one thought is quickly odious. We house with the insane, and must humor them; then conversation dies out. Once I took such delight in Montaigne, that I thought I should not need any other book; before that, in Shakspeare; then in Plutarch; then in Plotinus; at one time in Bacon; afterwards in Goethe; even in Bettine; but now I turn the pages of either of them languidly, whilst I still cherish their genius." This is Emerson's longer version of William Blake's apothegm, from *Milton*, 1810: "Time is the Mercy of Eternity." Gazziniga describes this experiment in *Who's in Charge?: Free Will and the Science of the Brain* (New York: Ecco, 2011), pp. 82–84. The quotation in which he explains why his theory "makes sense" is on p. 84. He mentions "fudging" on p. 86. I should mention that Adam Gopnik, in his *New Yorker* article "Mindless: The New Neuro-Skeptics" (September 9, 2013), notes the following: "There was [once] the left-right brain split, which insisted on a far neater break within our heads . . . than is now believed to exist." This doesn't fit my narrative at all. Therefore I say: Take it up with Gazzaniga; he's the scientist, and a big-shot one at that, with all sorts of legitimate awards and honors, and his research is recent. Likely the left-brain/right-brain theory didn't fit Gopnik's narrative, so he dismissed it in passing. Since my narrative is not such, at this time, one that encourages rigorous research—the urge to get to the bottom of things—I can't be bothered to sort out what's au courant in science.

15.

I draw my account of Peirce entirely from Joseph Brent's definitive biography *Charles Sanders Peirce: A Life* (Indianapolis: Indiana University Press, 1993). We now realize that Peirce was one of the towering geniuses in thought and one of the most influential figures in twentieth-century philosophy, semiotics, and science. With William James, he created pragmatism (Peirce called it pragmaticism), the major American contribution to Western thought and still a vital vision. He created a theory of signs that informed many distinguished literary theorists, such as Umberto Eco. And he was one of the first scientists to envision what we now call chaos theory, or nonlinear dynamics. In *Objective Knowledge: An Evolutionary Approach*, rev. ed. (Oxford: Oxford University Press, 1972), p. 215, Karl R. Popper writes, "I believe Peirce was right in holding that all clocks are clouds, to some considerable degree—even the most precise of clocks."

16.

The quote from Hume comes from *A Treatise of Human Nature*, ed. David Fate Norton and Mary J. Norton, intro. David Fate Norton (New York: Oxford University Press, 2000), p. 163. Dennett's essay appears in *The Times Literary Supplement*, September 16–22, 1988. The best sources for Ricoeur's basic views are *Oneself as Another*, trans. Kathleen Blamey (Chicago: Chicago University Press, 1992); *Time and Narrative*, 3 vols., trans. Kathleen McLaughlin and Dave Pellauer (Chicago: Chicago University Press, 1990); and *The Rule of Metaphor: Multi-disciplinary Studies of the Creation of Meaning in Language*, trans. Robert Czerny (Toronto: University of Toronto Press, 1981). In my discussion here, I draw from the long entry on Ricoeur in *The Stanford Encyclopedia of Philosophy* (www.plato.stanford/entries/).

17.

I am still closely in touch with Baxter (whose name is really not Baxter). We talked just this past weekend about my including this narrative in the book. I asked him why he thought we had done this. He claimed that we had done it because we liked exerting power over others, scripting the moment, directing the action, duping at will. He is a philosopher by training and trade, and so he must know. When we undertook this loopy excursion, I thought that the Bee Gees and the film *Saturday Night Fever* were silly—nothing but naive camp, though I didn't know that concept, not having read Susan Sontag then. But now I find that the Bee Gees are brilliant, not only for their harmonies and energy but also for the rich melancholia underneath the falsetto, especially in songs like "Nights on Broadway" and "Tragedy." Same goes for *Saturday Night Fever.* John Travolta gives one of the more vital performances in movie history, and the picture features a Martin Scorsese-esque urban darkness. *Wizard of Oz*: remember that Dorothy's last name is Gale. She wants that twister to blow away the Kansas farm where she is ignored, babied, betrayed, disappointed, bored, and it does. When she says there's no place like home at the movie's conclusion, she's lying. The surreal theatrics of Oz is where it's at: reality so real it's magic. (I don't know what that means, but it has a nice koanlike ring.) I should say that I'm borrowing the interpretation of the film, especially the take on Dorothy's last name, from Salman Rushdie's wonderful little book *The Wizard of Oz* (London: BFI Film Classics, 2008).

18.

Ginsberg's "Howl" still reads best in the little City Lights volume, pocket size, published by Lawrence Ferlinghetti in 1956, and introduced by William Carlos Williams. The beautiful lines on Ginsberg's mother, Naomi, come from his elegy for her, "Kaddish," completed in 1959, published in 1961. I realized the importance of Dadaism for my book on fakeness while reading Greil Marcus's account of Dada's influence on the punk movement in *Lipstick Traces: A Secret History of the Twentieth Century.* My brief discussion of Dadaism is based on Marcus's book. Calvin Tomkins's *Duchamp: A Biography* (1996) is an excellent source on the artist. I learned of Duchamp's habit of packing lightly in "Ready-Made Genius," Deborah Solomon's December 1996 review of Tomkins's biography in *The New York Times.* Comte de Lautréamont's famous line can be found in his *Maldoror and Poems*, trans. and intro. Paul Knight (New York: Penguin, 1988). Breton's quotation appears in his *Manifestoes of Surrealism*, trans. Richard Seaver and Helen R. Lane (Ann Arbor: University of Michigan Press, 1969). The situationist passage on "moments of rupture" comes from an unsigned essay in the magazine *Situationist International* 4 (June 1960), titled "The Theory of Moments and the Construction of Situations," pp. 10–11, in *Theory of the Dérive and Other Situationist Writings on the City*, ed. Libero Andreotti and Xavier Costa

(Barcelona: Museu d'Art Contemporani de Barcelona, 1997), pp. 100–101. The quotation from Greil Marcus on the "politics of freeze-out" comes from his *Lipstick Traces*.

19.

When Corso visited the class, he asked who in the group wrote poetry. I and a few others raised hands. Corso scanned the volunteers, lighted on me, and said, "That one's got the looks for it." I still don't know if this was a compliment or an insult.

20.

The quotations from Borges's "Funes, the Memorious" are from his *Ficciones*, ed. Anthony Kerrigan, trans. Anthony Bonner (New York: Grove, 1994), p. 14.

21.

In his *Confessions of an English Opium Eater*, De Quincey famously wrote about a dream spawned by a strange visit from a Malaysian; the description concludes in Dadaesque surrealism: "I was kissed with cancerous kisses, by crocodiles, and laid, confounded with unutterable slimy things, amongst reeds and Nilotic mud" (*Confessions of an English Opium Eater* [New York: Penguin, 2003] p. 82). I say with embarrassment that most of my first drafts sound like awful imitations of such crazed, mellifluous prose, so enamored am I of Romantic purplishness.

22.

I learned about Schopenhauer's canine affectation in David E. Cartwright's *Historical Dictionary of Schopenhauer's Philosophy* (New York: Scarecrow Press, 2004), p. 136. Schopenhauer's discussion of the *principium individuationis* can be found in his *World as Will and Representation*, vol. 1, trans. E.F.J. Payne (Mineola, NY: Dover, 1966), pp. 111–27. I came across Schopenhauer's passage on music, which appears in *The World as Will and Representation*, in *A Companion to Schopenhauer*, ed. Bart Vandenabeele (Cambridge, UK: Blackwell-Wiley, 2012), p. 169.

23.

I found Nietzsche's description of his initial exposure to Schopenhauer in *A Companion to Schopenhauer*, p. 335. Nietzsche's passage on truth and lie can be found in *The Portable Nietzsche*, ed. and trans. Walter Kaufmann (New York: Penguin, 1977), p. 46. When I was in college and deep in Nietzsche, I discovered the essential role Kaufmann played in presenting Nietzsche to Anglo-American readers in an accurate light. I also found out—this was in 1989—Nietzsche's profound influence on the important French theorists: Derrida, Foucault, et al. A friend of mine wrote me a startlingly Dadaesque poem at the time: "Kaufmann was wrong."

24.

I first learned of Vaihinger during a conversation with Robert D. Richardson, Jr., the biographer of William James (as well as of Emerson and Thoreau). He told me that Vaihinger's thought was very similar to that of James, the progenitor of American pragmatism.

25.

I have told the story of my time at West Point in *The Mercy of Eternity: A Memoir of Depression and Grace* and *Everyone Loves a Good Train Wreck: Why We Can't Look Away*. As I said, I tell it here again from another angle—with the focus mostly on Murray. I also like telling the story. Please don't accuse me of being Jonah Lehrer and plagiarizing myself.

26.

Thomson's book *The Big Sleep* was published in 1997 by the British Film Institute, out of London. Thomson illuminates what I have always loved about Hawks's films, regardless of genre. They seem to be less about narrative and more about finding interesting ways simply to keep the conversation going. This is true even in Hawks's pulpiest picture, codirected with Christian Nyby, *The Thing from Another World* (1951). If you can make chitchat between Kenneth Tobey and Margaret Sheridan casual yet interesting, you can do anything.

27.

I draw my information on Grant from Richard Schickel's *Cary Grant: A Celebration* (New York: Little, Brown, 2009), Marc Eliot's *Cary Grant: A Biography* (New York: Three Rivers Press, 2005), and Graham McCann's *Cary Grant* (New York: Columbia University Press, 1998). Some excerpts from this discussion come from my article "Cary Grant: Prince of Denmark," *Bright Lights Film Journal* 68 (May 2010). Grant's lines about the difficulty of playing yourself are from Nancy Nelson, *Evenings with Cary Grant* (New York: Warner, 1993), p. 55; quoted in McCann, p. 166. Whenever I write about living LARGE, as Hamlet and Grant do, I have in the back of my mind lines from Clark Gable, as Peter Warne, in *It Happened One Night*, where he confesses to Claudette Colbert, playing Elie Andrews, that he has thought mightily about falling in love, and making "some girl very happy." He says that he and she would visit a Pacific island where

> you and the moon and the water all become one. You feel you're part of something big and marvelous. That's the only place to live. The stars are so close over your head you feel you could reach up and stir them around. Certainly, I've been thinking about it. Boy, if I could ever find a girl who was hungry for those things.

Here pop culture, bordering on sentimental schlock, approaches art, rising to a pitch not quite as high as Emerson but pretty close. That Clark Gable voices this lovely passage—which expresses my hunger for something real more startlingly and intensely almost than even Keats—is uncanny: unsettling and vital at once. I think Gable would be an utter overbearing idiot in person, and usually he is uninteresting to me in his pictures, save for this one fantastic moment in *It Happened One Night*, and two more. In *Teacher's Pet* (in which his love interest, Doris Day, is *way* too young for him), Gable shows the profoundly hungover character played by Gig Young (who would later murder his wife, allegedly, and then kill himself, and who played in the best *Twilight Zone* episode ever, "Walking Distance," about how the dreams of childhood are more real than adult bruises) how to make a martini: you rub the cork from the vermouth bottle around the inner edge of the shaker. And in

The Misfits, Gable's last film, he asserts, while freeing a mustang he has just brutally lassoed, "I'm finished with [capturing mustangs]. It's like roping a dream now. I just gotta find another way to be alive, that's all. If there is one anymore." "A way to be alive." "Somebody that's real." I want these things, too, Clark, with all my heart, but I'm not willing to go as far as you did. You did your own stunts for *The Misfits*, disdainful of fakery, "including," Wikipedia says, "being dragged about 400 feet (120 m) across the dry lake bed at more than 30 miles per hour (48 km/h)." You were fifty-nine, and had probably hardly worked out a day in your life, maybe a push-up or two. After your third wife, Carole Lombard, died in a plane crash near Las Vegas, you flew to where the plane went down and studied the mangled, charred bodies of the victims until you recognized the woman you loved. You really loved her, I believe, finding in her the fleshing out of your dream girl in *It Happened*. Of Carole you sweetly said, as though acting a line from one of those zany romantic comedies of the 1930s (comedies of remarriage, according to Stanley Cavell), "You can trust that little screwball with your life or your hopes or your weaknesses." You enlisted in the U.S. Army soon after this tragedy, in 1942, and actually trained yourself to be an aerial bomber. (So you *did* exercise, at least in basic training.) As captain, you flew five combat missions, almost got shot in the head. Hitler, it was said, valued you most among American actors, and offered a large reward to the soldier who could deliver you to him alive, unwounded.

28.

I found both these quotes from Montaigne in Sarah Bakewell's *How to Live: Or a Life of Montaigne in One Question and Twenty Attempts at an Answer* (New York: Other Press, 2010), pp. 125, 32.

29.

I found the account of the inception of *The Razor's Edge* in K. Tighe's "Found in Translation: John Byrum Revisits The Razor's Edge and Bill Murray's Dramatic Debut," *San Francisco Bay Guardian*, August 8, 2006. Timothy White's article on Murray appeared in *The New York Times* on November 20, 1988.

30.

Sontag's "Notes on Camp" can be found in *Against Interpretation and Other Essays* (New York: Picador, 2001), pp. 275–92.

31.

In *The Waste Land*, his poem of 1922, T. S. Eliot has the thunder say "DA" three times. A lesson follows each sounding. Eliot draws the lessons and the thunder sound from *Bṛihadaranyaka Upanishad*.

32.

The quotation of Bhikkhu Bodhi is from his introduction to *The Middle Length Discourses of the Buddha: A Translation of the Majjhima Nikaya*, trans. Bhikkhu Bodhi and Bhikkhu Nanomali (Somerville, MA: Wisdom Publications, 1995), p. 26. I cite Edward Conze's translation of the Heart Sutra, found in *Buddhist Wisdom: The Diamond Sutra and the Heart Sutra*, trans. and comm. Edward Conze, pref. Judith Simmer-Brown (New York: Vintage, 2001), pp. 76–77. My discussion of the Buddhist void is based largely on Alan Watts's *The Way of Zen* (New York: Vintage, 1999), especially pp. 60–65, as well as on D. T. Suzuki's *Manual of Zen Buddhism* (New York: Grove Press, 1994), especially pp. 29–31 and 70–75. For an excellent discussion of the Jewel Net of Indra, see Francis H. Cook's *Hua-Yen Buddhism: The Jewel Net of Indra* (University Park, PA: Penn State University Press, 2001). Watts discusses letting go of permanence in a more secular form in *The Wisdom of Insecurity: A Message for an Age of Anxiety* (New York: Vintage, 2011).

33.

I borrow the idea that truth "happens" to an idea from Richardson's *William James*, p. 486. The Posnock quote comes from *The Trial of Curiosity: Henry James, William James, and the Challenge of Modernity* (New York: Oxford University Press, 1991), p. 172. I found the passage on James's struggle with the horrid shape in Richardson, pp. 117–18. Henry senior's description of his own battle with psychological terror I also found in Richardson, p. 18. James's passage on *willing* free will appears in Richardson, p. 120. I love that Henry senior called Emerson a "man without a handle."

34.

I came across this incident in James's life in Richardson's *William James: In the Maelstrom of American Modernism* (Boston: Mariner Books, 2007), p. 3. You can read about Lohmann in the February 2013 *Smithsonian*, in an article by Megan Gambino, titled "With Biodesign, Life Is Not Only the Subject of Art, But the Medium Too."

35.

In my discussion of Mesmer, I mainly draw from Robert Darnton's *Mesmerism and the End of the Enlightenment in France* (Cambridge: Harvard University Press, 2009), pp. 3–65. The *Radiolab* episode was the first one from season three; it aired on May 18, 2007. I discuss Descartes's automaton at length in *The Melancholy Android: On the Psychology of Sacred Machines* (Albany, NY: SUNY Press, 2006), pp. 89–96.

36.

Several publications mention that Dillard admitted that she borrowed the image of the tomcat. I first came across the incident in Ralph Keyes's *The Post-Truth Era: Dishonesty and Deception in Contemporary Life* (New York: St. Martin's, 2004), pp. 160–62. Maureen Dowd's article, "Oprah's Bunk Club," appears in the January 28, 2006, edition of *The New York Times*. Larry King suggested that Oprah annihilated Frey in the May 1, 2007, episode of *CNN Larry King Live*. King was interviewing Winfrey about the Frey incident. Sara Nelson's review appears in *Publishers Weekly* (April 14, 2008). For my discussion of how genre affects a work's veracity, I am deeply indebted to Siska Lyssens's "Fiction in Autobiographical Life Writing: Self-representation in James Frey's *A Million Little Pieces*," a master's thesis she completed at the University of Ghent in 2008 and 2009.

37.

The Borges quotation from "Pierre Menard, Author of the Quixote" appears in Borges's *Ficciones*, pp. 52–53. The quotation from Robert Hass comes from his introduction to *The Selected Poetry of Rainer Maria Rilke*, trans. and ed. Stephen Mitchell (New York: Vintage, 1989), p. xxxviii.

38.

The books growing from my obsession with the uncanny are as follows: *The Spiritual History of Ice, Coleridge's Melancholia, The Melancholy Android, The Strange World of David Lynch, Against Happiness,* and *My Business Is to Create.* I have written about the importance of my Appalachian heritage before, mainly in *Everyone Loves a Good Train Wreck.* Here I express a deeper appreciation of this past.

39.

The Picasso quote is from "Picasso Speaks," *The Arts* (May 1923), p. 315. The Camus: I can't find the source anywhere, but it's listed on hundreds of quotable quote pages throughout the Internet—which doesn't mean he actually said it. The Wilde is easy to find; it is in *The Artist as Critic: Critical Writings of Oscar Wilde,* ed. Richard Ellmann (Chicago: University of Chicago Press, 1982), p. 389. I discovered *Time*'s 2009 poll on Stewart's perceived honesty in Jason Linkins's "Online Poll: Jon Stewart Is America's Most Trusted Newsman," Huffington Post, August 22, 2009. I learned of the 2004 Pew survey on the alleged veracity of *The Daily Show* and *SNL* in Bootie Cosgrove-Mather's "Young Get News from Comedy Central," cbsnews.com, March 1, 2004. I found the stats on the knowledge levels of Stewart and Colbert fans in Steve Benen's "Political Animal" column in *The Washington Monthly,* April 21, 2010. In understanding why Stewart and Colbert are trustworthy, I benefited from Carolyn Shanahan's interview with Professor Adam Lifshey in *The Hoya* (January 27, 2009), Georgetown University's student paper (www.the hoya.com/its-funny-because-its-true-professor-examines-role-of -satire-media/). Another helpful article was Ronald E. Riggio's "Cutting-Edge Leadership: Why Jon Stewart Is the Most Trusted Man in America," on *Psychology Today*'s website, posted on July 24, 2009 (www .psychologytoday.com/blog/cutting-edge-leadership/200907/why -jon-stewart-is-the-most-trusted-man-in-america/). The Wallace Stevens quote appears in his *Opus Posthumous: Poems, Plays, Prose* (New York: Vintage, 1990). My discussion of the pressures of reality and imagination is based on Stevens's essay "The Noble Rider and the Sound of Words," in *The Necessary Angel* (New York: Vintage, 1965), pp. 1–36.

40.

Woolf's passage on how we endure appears in *To the Lighthouse*, intro. Eudora Welty (New York: Harcourt Brace Jovanovich, 1989), p. 126. Mr. Ramsay stumbles over Mrs. Ramsay's death on p. 128. Other Woolf quotes: "ghostly roll of drums," p. 16; "taking out of pipes," p. 15; "insensibility of nature," p. 138; "little daily miracles," p. 161; "I have had my vision," p. 209.

41.

Ruskin's line on the Venice moon can be found in his diary, May 6, 1841. I found the quotation in John Batchelor's *John Ruskin: A Life* (New York: Carroll and Graf, 2000), p. 47. The quotation from Browne appears in *Religio Medici and Urne-Buriall*, ed. Stephen Greenblatt and Ramie Targoff (New York: New York Review of Books Classics, 2012), p. 134. The Emerson quotation comes from his 1841 essay "Circles."

42.

This section is mostly excerpted from my essay "The Most Dangerous Hobby in the World: Film Collecting in the Digital Age," *Virginia Quarterly Review* (Spring 2009).

43.

For a discussion of Romantic irony and Lynch, see my *The Strange World of David Lynch: Transcendental Irony from* Eraserhead *to* Mulholland Dr. (New York: Continuum, 2007). Excellent sources for learning about Romantic irony are Anne K. Mellor's *English Romantic Irony* (Cambridge, MA: Harvard University Press, 1980) and Frederick Garber's *Self, Text, and Romantic Irony: The Example of Byron* (Princeton, NJ: Princeton University Press, 1988). As I say, I've written about this idea before—I find it so fascinating and powerful—not only in my Lynch book, but also in *Secret Cinema* and *Against Happiness*. I am somewhat obsessed with the notion.

44.

For the passage from Farber, see "White Elephant vs. Termite Art," *Film Culture* 27 (1962), pp. 9–13. I first picked up on the idea from reading

Greil Marcus's *The Doors: A Lifetime of Listening to Five Mean Years* (New York: Public Affairs, 2011), p. 4. I am ashamed to admit that English professors are notorious for trying verbally to cut down writers far superior to themselves. I've actually heard my colleagues say: "Dickinson: a little flat, don't you think?" and "Emerson's really just rhetoric."

45.

For Nochimson on the marketplace, see *David Lynch Swerves: Uncertainty from* Lost Highway *to* Inland Empire (Austin: University of Texas Press, 2014), p. 4. Her discussion of "free flows of energy" appears on p. 90.

46.

The David Foster Wallace quote is in *This Is Water: Some Thoughts, Delivered on a Significant Occasion, About Living a Compassionate Life* (New York: Little, Brown, 2009), pp. 89–90. For metamodernism, see Timotheus Vermeulen and Robin van den Akker's "Notes on Metamodernism," *Journal of Aesthetics and Culture* 2 (November 15, 2010), pp. 1–13. Purdy was featured as a hero against our Seinfeldian 1990s culture of irony in the September 5, 1999, edition of *The New York Times Magazine*. He was twenty-four, recently graduated from Harvard, and the author of *For Common Things: Irony, Trust, and Commitment in America Today* (New York: Vintage, 2000). Depressed, sarcastic, envious, resentful, threatened, charmed, disgusted, I *hated* him. Don't know how I feel now. But I know he teaches at Duke's law school, about eighty minutes' drive from where I live. I bet he could come up here to Winston-Salem and kick my ass if he wanted. He grew up on a West Virginia farm and is probably strong and healthy.

47.

I hope that this time I finally get the deepest meaning of this period of my life, and can put it to rest. I've also used the old gravity parable before, too, and will again. I like having thought of it so much.

48.

Sometimes I pretend to be Christian Bale, as he appears in his roles in a composite way, when I need to be insouciant, aloof, raspy, and smart.

49.

I found this story of St. Francis in Harriet Rubin's lovely *Dante in Love: The World's Greatest Poem and How It Made History* (New York: Simon & Schuster, 2005), p. 52.

50.

This *Radiolab* episode is titled "The Fact of the Matter." It is episode one of season eleven, and it first aired on September 24, 2012.

ACKNOWLEDGMENTS

I would like to thank Christopher Schelling, my agent, for helping me to focus my ideas in the early stages of writing this book. I also benefited from conversations with my friend and former colleague John McNally. Phil Arnold, my longtime boon companion, read the manuscript carefully and offered very insightful—as well as witty and supportive—advice. I dedicate this book to him. I am once again grateful to my publisher, Sarah Crichton. This is the third book I've done with her, and she remains an excellent editor and a pleasure to work with. I can also say that it has been a pleasure to work with Sarah's extremely accomplished assistant, Marsha Sasmor. Conversations with several other close friends—Dennis Sampson, Andy Lester-Niles, Brian Lefevre, Angus MacLachlan, Terry Price, John McElwee, Joel Tauber, and Kevin Calhoun—have proved most fruitful. Finally, I am grateful to my wife, Sandi Hamilton, who was closely involved with this book from beginning to end and helped me make it much clearer and more humane than it would otherwise have been.